Walks & Easy Hikes
in
Rocky Mountain
National Park

Text and Photographs by
Patrick Soran

Altitude Publishing

Publication Information

Altitude Publishing Ltd.

Head Office: 1500 Railway Avenue
Canmore, Alberta T1W 1P6
www.altitudepublishing.com

Cataloging in Publication Data

Patrick Soran1953-
Walks and Easy Hikes in Rocky Mountain National Park (An Altitude SuperGuide)
Includes index.
ISBN 1-55265-041-3
1. Hiking-Colorado-Rocky Mountain National Park--Guidebooks.
2) Trails-Colorado-Rocky Mountain National Park--Guidebooks.
3) Rocky Mountain National Park (Colo.)-Guidebooks. I. Title. II. Series: Altitude superguide
GV199.42.C62R627 2002 796.51'09788'69
C2002-910150-6

Printed and bound in Western Canada by Friesen Printers, Altona, Manitoba.

Altitude GreenTree Program

Altitude Publishing will plant twice as many trees as were used in the manufacturing of this product.

We acknowledge the financial support of the Government of Canada through the Book Publishing Industry Development Program (BPIDP) for our publishing activities.

Project Development

Associate Publishers	Dan Klinglesmith
	Patrick Soran
Design/Layout	Patrick Soran
Editor	Dan Klinglesmith
Maps	Hermien Schuttenbeld

A Note from the Publisher

The world described in *Altitude SuperGuides* is a unique and fascinating place. It is a world filled with surprise and discovery, beauty and enjoyment, questions and answers. It is a world of people, cities, landscape, animals and wilderness as seen through the eyes of those who live in, work with, and care for this world. The process of describing this world is also a means of defining ourselves.

It is also a world of relationship, where people derive their meaning from a deep and abiding contact with the land—as well as from each other. And it is this sense of relationship that guides all of us at Altitude to ensure that these places continue to survive and evolve in the decades ahead.

Altitude SuperGuides are books intended to be used, as much as read. Like the world they describe, Altitude SuperGuides are evolving, adapting and growing. Please write to us with your comments and observations, and we will do our best to incorporate your ideas into future editions of these books.

Stephen Hutchings
Publisher

Photographs

Front Cover: Patrick Soran
Back Cover: Patrick Soran

Contents

How to use this book

There are several ways to select a hike from this book. The table on page nine provides lots of useful information to help find exactly the walk or hike you're after. If you want a short or flat hike, simply study the distance or elevation columns. If you know you're going to be in a certain area of the park, study the trailhead map to select one of the hikes in that neighborhood. One of the most spontaneous ways is simply to pick one of the pictures in the book that appeals to you and take that hike. All the pictures in this book were taken from the trails described.

More!

Some of the hikes in this book are actually portions of longer, steeper hikes. When this is the case, and the extended hike is reasonable, we add a short description of it.

Walks & Easy Hikes is organized with the following color scheme:

Introduction . . . . ▭   Reference and Biography . . . . ▬

Walks & Easy Hikes . . . . ▬

Introduction

Elk on the alpine tundra

T he walks and easy hikes described in this book will take you into every one of the ecological habitats, climatic zones and geologic types which make Rocky Mountain National Park one of the most popular hiking locations in the country. The hikes here will take you to pleasurable

picnic places, vast vista viewpoints, terrific terra, fabulous forests, and wonderful wildlife.

You don't need to be a gnarly backwoods hiker to have a significant wilderness experience in the great Colorado outdoors. All you need do is park the car nearly anywhere in Rocky Mountain National Park, pack a few essentials and take a few steps. It sometimes comes as a shock to find out how nearby the wilderness really is, but on many of the trails described here, simply putting one foot in front of the other carries

you very quickly into a land of wild and serenity-inducing beauty.

What does "Walks and Easy Hikes" mean?

What do we mean when we say "walks" or "easy hikes?" No hike in this book is longer than seven miles round-trip and none asks you to conquer more than 1,000 feet in elevation. We take a "walk" to be more or less a stroll of less than a mile with very little elevation gain. By "Easy Hike,"

we mean a hike with some elevation gain and a bit more length; a very few of these contain some rock scrambling or a stretch of rugged trail.

There are about 60 trails in Rocky which are less than seven miles long and climb less than 1,000 feet; that is to say, they fit our technical definition of a walk or easy hike. We didn't include many of them here for a couple of reasons. First, many of these don't have any facilities. We wanted to get into the wild, but we didn't see why there couldn't be a bathroom

Left: Wildflowers accent both rocks and aspen along the trail to Cub Lake

nearby. Plus we wanted a trail-head with a map and some parking. We wanted a definite trail as well, something designed and maintained by the Park Service, not a scramble across a rock field. And while we broke all theses rule for an exceptional hike or two—Old Ute Trail, for instance—we wanted to get into the great wide open and not kill ourselves doing it.

In addition, and perhaps more importantly, we looked for something wonderful about each hike—a classic moment.

Imagine hiking through a dreary dark forest for 45 minutes. All around are nothing but straight-as-needle trees with gray bark and no undergrowth. Suddenly you turn a corner and before you stretches a vast high-alpine valley bursting with sunshine

and hundreds of millions of wildflowers. You stop to stare, elated. That's a classic moment.

Each of the hikes in this book has some experience which makes it a classic. Some are grand vistas; some are quiet realizations. One is nothing more than a thicket of ferns deep in one of those forests, a place of unexpected serenity.

The first 28 hikes in this book are scattered along the eastern side of Rocky Mountain National Park. This is Colorado's finest region of wide, glacier-carved valleys—called parks. We'll explore these grassy areas on several walks as well as getting right up to the edge of a couple of rivers, feeling the splash of waterfalls and climbing high into alpine areas dotted with pristine lakes. There are

sprightly aspen forests to explore as well as ponderosa pine to sit under and some immense boulders which are perfect for a picnic.

The next three hikes track into the alpine tundra. Rocky has one of the largest areas of tundra in the world. And it's easy to get to. Hike 30 is a must-do which takes you to a high vantage point overlooking much of the park.

Hikes 32 through 37 delve into the Kawunechee Valley, the heart of the Colorado River. The high, wet grasslands of 38, 40, and 42 are moose country. And 37, the Coyote Valley Trail, is wide-open and wonderful.

Native Americans in the Park

Trail Ridge Road isn't the first highway to cut through the regions of Rocky Mountain National Park. Ute and Arapaho passed this way often on their migrations from the Great Plains to the immense valleys high in the mountains; valleys such as North Park and South Park.

There isn't any indication that these natives lived within the boundaries of Rocky. However, both tribes did extensive hunting and fishing in these parts apparently. The Ute lived on the west side, the Arapaho on the east. Both went back and forth across the park hunting for deer, elk and a species of bison which occupied the area.

Interestingly, they used trails

very similar to the ones we use today to get across. In fact, it is believed that the trail which runs up Forest Canyon—now called the Old Ute Trail—was the way they actually traveled from one side of the park to the other. They would move west up the Ute Trail, then follow pretty closely what we now call Trail Ridge Road across the tundra, and then drop down into the Kawuneeche Valley much as the road now does from the Alpine Visitor Center to Poudre Lake.

How do we know that they used this route? Fire rings and arrowheads have been found.

The Utes and Arapaho had a long history of antagonism. They ambushed each other regularly

and fought tribal wars frequently, probably over hunting areas. One story has it they were fighting in the area of Grand Lake one summer. As the sun rose one morning it shown into fog on the lake and created eerie, ghostlike apparitions. Perhaps this explains why Native Americans have always called this Spirit Lake.

Another legend has it that the mountains were created in an effort to separate the Ute and Arapaho and keep them from fighting.

Litl' Bit awaits the next cowpoke

Do Not Disturb

Keeping Rocky Mountain National Park as pristine as it is calls for each of us as hikers and users of the park to make some efforts at preservation.

• **If you bring** something onto a trail, please carry it out—energy bar wrappers, picnic supplies, etc.

• **No matter how** desperate they look, those animals don't need to eat any human food. Look closely at these little beggars—squirrels and

Deer surprised near Ouzel Falls in the early morning

marmots are the worse—and you can easily see by how fat they are that they don't need handouts.

• **The restrooms are** there for a reason. As far as you think you are from a stream, using

a tree or bush may well contaminate the water.

• **The park would** have a lot more wild-flowers for everyone to enjoy if everyone would leave the ones we have alone.

• **Stay on the trail,** particularly in the tundra areas. These plants can take decades—dozens of decades—to recover from a single boot print.

7

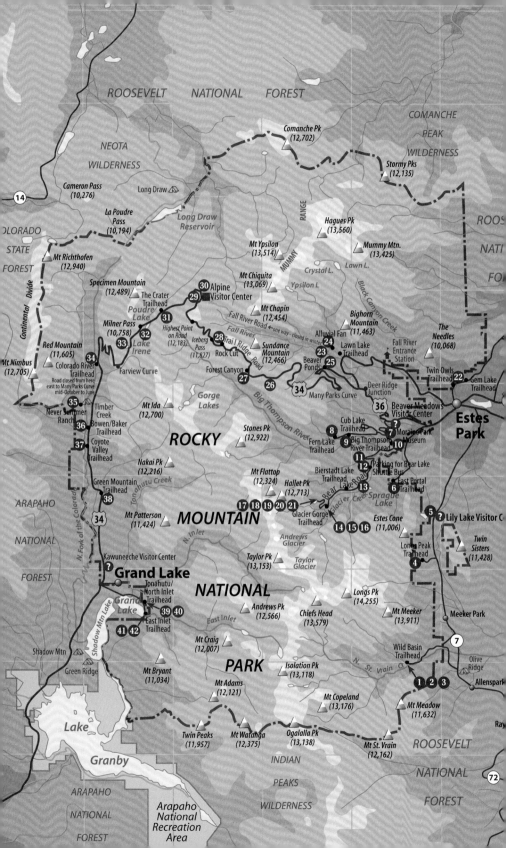

Walks & Easy Hikes in Rocky Mountain National Park

HIKE NAME	LENGTH (miles)	ELEVATION CHANGE	TEXT PAGE	MAP PAGE	CLASSIC MOMENT
1) Copeland Falls	0.3	15	13	14	Waterfall
2) Calypso Cascades	1.8	700	15	14	Sprightly Cascade
3) Ouzel Falls	2.7	950	16	14	Forest Regrowth
4) Eugenia Mine	1.4	500	17	20	Historic Mine
5) Lily Lake Loop	0.6	0.0	18	20	Lily Mtn. and Longs Peak Views
6) East Portal/YMCA	6.0	300	19	20	Aspen Groves
7) Moraine Park Museum	0.65	45	21	20	Park Vistas
8) The Pool/Fern Falls	1.7/2.7	250/650	22	24	The Pool and the falls
9) Cub Lake	2.3	540	23	24	Water lilies
10) Big Thompson River	0.25–5.0	0.0	25	20	Serene and lazy riverbed
11) Mill Creek Basin	1.6	600	26	32	Varied ecosystems
12) Bierstadt Lake	2.3	550	27	32	Up- and down-valley views
13) Sprague Lake Loop	0.5	0	28	32	Hallett Peak view
14) Alberta Falls	0.6	160	29	32	Valley views and falls
15) Mills Lake	2.5	700	31	32	The Best; vistas and lakes
16) The Loch	2.7	970	33	32	Alpine lake
17) Bear Lake Nature Trail	0.5	10	34	39	Glacially carved mountaintops
18) Nymph Lake	0.5	225	25	39	Hallett Peak reflected
19) Dream Lake	1.1	425	36	39	Perfect picnic rocks
20) Emerald Lake	1.8	605	37	39	Setting and subtle waterfalls
21) Haiyaha Lake	2.1	745	38	39	Massive rock falls
22) Gem Lake	1.8	910	40	39	Twin Owls formation/views
23) Fall River Trail	0.5-2.0	20	42	39	Quiet moment in a busy park
24) Alluvial Fan	0.5	50	43	39	Destructive force of nature
25) Beaver Ponds	0.25	10	44	39	How animals make a living
26) Ute Trail	2.0	150	49	50	Wide open wonder of tundra
27) Forest Canyon	0.25	15	51	50	Immense glacial valley
28) Rock Cut	0.5	250	52	50	Eerie rock formations
29) Fall River Pass	2.0	−476	53	50	Tiny alpine lakes
30) Alpine Ridge	0.5	150	55	50	Northern park views
31) The Crater	1.0	730	58	59	The Crater
32) Poudre Lake Walk	0.1	10	60	59	The lake's colorful water
33) Lake Irene	0.5	60	61	59	Perfect lake in perfect setting
34) Lulu City	3.7	350	62	63	Forest ferns/Colorado River
35) Never Summer Ranch	0.5	0.0	66	70	Old log buildings/history
36) Bowen/Baker Trail	1.0	50	67	70	Bubbling forest stream
37) Coyote Valley Trail	1.0	0.0	68	70	Broad valley vistas/info panels
38) Big Meadows	1.8	600	71	70	Lazy streams and the Meadow
39) Summerland Park	1.2	50	73	74	Easy walk/fun place to play
40) Cascade Falls	3.5	300	75	74	Lovely hike in aspen/falls
41) Adams Falls	0.3	79	76	74	The Falls
42) East Inlet Meadows	1.7	160	77	74	Meadow and moose

A Primer on Rocky Mountain National Park

Hosting nearly 3.5 million visitors per year Rocky Mountain National Park is among the most popular national parks in the nation. *Backpacker* magazine recognized it as being among the most hikeable. While it may seem big and complex, Rocky is easy to get around in and easy to enjoy.

Size:
• 415.2 square miles
• 265,727 acres

Founded:
Established on January 26, 1915 Rocky was the tenth addition to the national park system.

Elevations:
• Beaver Meadows Visitor Center: 7,840 feet above sea level
• Top of Trail Ridge Road: 12,183 feet above sea level
• Kawuneeche Visitor Center: 8,720 feet above sea level
• Highest Peak: Longs Peak: 14,255 feet above sea level, Colorado's 15th highest mountain

Peaks:
• 114 named peaks above 10,000 feet
• 60 peaks above 12,000 feet
• 20 peaks above 13,000 feet
• one peak above 14,000 feet

Number of Lakes: 150 (one for every 28 square miles)
Lakes with fish: 50
Bird Species: 260
Endangered Species present: Peregrine falcon
Animal Populations as of 1996:
• Bighorn sheep: 650

Animals
• Elk: 2,000 in winter; 3,500 in summer
• Mule deer: 250 in winter
• Black Bear: 30
Types of Trees, Flowers and Grasses: 1,105
Information Number:
The telephone number for Rocky Mountain National Park is (970) 586-1206.

Park Regulations:
• Pets are not allowed on hiking or nature trails or in the backcountry. Pets are allowed in established campgrounds, picnic areas, on roadways and in parking lots. They must be on a leash with a six-foot maximum length.
• Camping is allowed only in designated camping areas. Backcountry camping requires a permit.
• All vehicles must remain on roadways or in parking lots. No off-road driving is allowed. Parking is allowed only in designated areas. State seatbelt and child restraint laws apply to the Park.
• Do not feed or attempt to touch any living creature. Do not chase the wildlife. No hunting or harassing of wildlife is allowed.
• Do not pick wildflowers. Staying on trails protects the flora for others to enjoy. Regulations prohibit the disturbance or removal of public property.
• Bicycles are allowed only on designated roadways. Trail riding and backcountry riding are not allowed.

• Open containers of alcohol are not allowed in cars while on the roads or in parking lots. State laws regarding alcohol apply within the boundaries of Rocky Mountain National Park.

Giardia
Although the waters in Rocky look harmless, delicious even, many streams and lakes contain a microscopic organism called *Giardia lamblia*. Within a few days of ingestion these may cause diarrhea, bloating, cramps and weight loss. A doctor's treatment is required. Boil water for five to 10 minutes prior to drinking.

Altitude Troubles
Symptoms of altitude sickness include shortness of breath, headache, tiredness, nasal congestion, dizziness and nausea. If symptoms persist or worsen go to a lower elevation and consult a physician. The best way to avoid altitude sickness is to acclimatize for a couple days.

Hypothermia
Wind, wet and cold can cause the body to loose its warmth quickly. Its temperature can drop to unsafe levels. Symptoms include shivering and disorientation. Always carry layers of clothing and rain gear when hiking. If you show symptoms, get to a warmer place as quickly as possible.

Sun Exposure
The ultraviolet rays of the sun burn with particular intensity at higher elevations. Protect skin with long pants and long sleeved shirts. Wear plenty of sunscreen and shade your eyes.

A Primer on Rocky Mountain National Park

Ticks

Ticks are cold-blooded parasites which thrive in brush, grass and woody areas from February until mid-July. Tuck trouser cuffs into boots, inspect your clothes, scalp and skin often and use a repellent. If you find a tick on your skin, pull it straight out using tweezers. Remove the body and the entire head.

Newsletter

The park's newsletter—*High Country Headlines*—is packed full with useful visitor information, as well as up to date information regarding guided hikes and other activities. Look for it in visitor centers or ask for one when you enter the park.

Food and Lodging

Food is available at the Alpine Visitor Center and the Fall River Visitor Center. No lodging is available in the park, however both Estes Park and Grand Lake offer a wide selection of lodging options.

Vapor Lock

Cars adjusted to lower altitudes often experience vapor lock at higher elevations. Cars may have trouble starting, the engine runs less smoothly and there is a loss of engine power. One good preventative is not to run the air conditioning. Another is to stay in a

An easy hike to Dream Lake

lower gear while climbing. At the first sign of stalling shift into neutral and give the engine some gas. If the car does stall coast to a safe spot and let the engine cool. Be careful not to flood it on restart.

Emergency Phones

Emergency phones are located at Bear Lake parking lot, Lawn Lake Trailhead, Longs Peak ranger station and Wild Basin ranger station.

Lightning

Lightning is a frequent and dangerous occurrence in Rocky. Stay off ridges and peaks and avoid lone objects such as large rocks or trees. Move to lower elevations if a storm threatens. If you get caught in a storm, crouch low with your hands around your knees.

Lost Children

Give children who are old enough to understand what they are doing a whistle to blow in case they get lost. Teach kids to stay put if they get lost.

Ice Fields

Do not attempt to climb across ice fields. They may not be as stable as they appear.

Bears

Bears are dangerous. Make plenty of noise while hiking to scare them off. If you encounter a bear on a hike, talk gently to it while backing away. Avoid eye contact.

Dressing for Rocky

A layered dressing strategy will help assure your comfort in any number of the different weather conditions that Rocky can dish up. Be certain to carry gear, storms can move fast, particularly

Reaching Rocky

The telephone number for Rocky Mountain National Park is (970) 586-1206.

Copeland Falls

~ 1 ~ Copeland Falls

Fast Facts

An easy walk deep into a Colorado forest. finishing with a rollicking waterfall

Length: 0.3 miles each way
Elevation Change: 15 feet
Map on Page: 14
Designation: Walk
Amenities: Ranger station, restrooms, wheelchair accessible
Trailhead: Wild Basin Ranger Station: On Colorado Highway 7, south of Estes Park approximately 13 miles, take the Wild Basin turn off into the park. Pass through the entrance station and follow the road approximately 2 miles to the ranger station.

While the aspen-lined, two-mile long gravel road leading to the parking for this stroll feels narrow, it offers a number of places to pull over and take short walks. Many people take a walk or short hike, then spread out a meal and enjoy the afternoon.

Parking for the Copeland Falls walk also accommodates Calypso Cascades and Ouzel Falls. Restrooms and picnic tables are available.

Head for the south end of the parking lot. Cross Hunter's Creek on a sturdy wooden bridge. Within a few feet, you've left the noise and bustle of the parking area behind and you're walking a broad, well-maintained path.

Swathes of aspen mix with fir and pine trees. Keep an eye open for wildflowers—wild rose and yellow wallflowers.

As you stroll, you'll begin to hear the noise of North St. Vrain Creek carving its way through Wild Basin. The urge to leave the trail and rush down to the rocks becomes almost overwhelming. Surrender and you'll find yourself scrabbling across big boulders and experiencing the cool rush of the water.

If you stay on the trail, you'll find a sign marking the falls at 0.3 miles. Turn left and follow this short trail down to the rocks.

A geologic shift dropped the valley here a few feet and a wedge of granite boulders piled up.

More!
Take Hikes Two and Three.

Left: A father and son enjoy a quiet moment together on the shore of Dream Lake

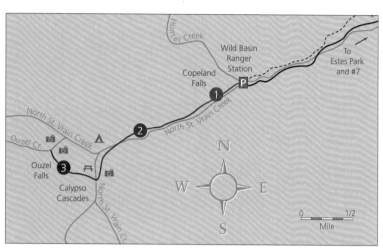

1

Copeland
Falls

2

Calypso
Cascades

3

Ouzel Falls

Walking to Preserve the Park

It sounds like a cliché, but if we don't protect Rocky Mountain National Park every time we use it, it will be degraded for those who follow.

Here are some guidelines to help preserve Rocky.

• Follow the Rules
The parks rules and regulations are meant to serve all of its users and protect the park's resources over the long haul.

• Do Not Feed the Animals
After you've taken a hike or two, and fallen in love with Rocky, you'll be shocked when you see people luring squirrels with nuts and candy. It's not good for the animals, which is not good for the park.

• Please Don't Pick the Flowers
The reason we don't see carpets of flowers nowadays is

On the trail to The Loch

because they've been picked by folks who got here before us. At least we can save what's left for whoever follows us.

• Stay on the Trails
Okay, you're going to crawl across the rocks to get to a picnic spot. No biggie if you're in the forest. But if you're up in the Alpine Tundra, stepping onto plants off the trail can mean that those plants may not grow again for decades. And if you cut off the switchbacks it means erosion and shorter life spans for the trail and the plantlife that keeps it entertaining.

• Pack in; Pack out
If you carry it in, please pack it out.

Wild Basin from the trail to Calypso Cascades

~ 2 ~ Calypso Cascades

Fast Facts

In addition to experiencing many waterfalls and cascades, a sense of being deep in the heart of Mother Nature accompanies this easy hike along a rushing mountain stream.

Length: 1.8 miles each way
Elevation Change: 700 feet
Map on Page: 14
Designation: Easy Hike
Amenities: Ranger station, restrooms
Trailhead: Wild Basin Ranger Station: On Colorado Highway 7, south of Estes Park approximately 13 miles, take the Wild Basin turn off into the park. Pass through the entrance station and follow the road approximately 2 miles to the ranger station.

Follow the wide trail to Copeland Falls, then continue up the trail. This well-maintained walkway parallels North St. Vrain Creek. Creeks like this carve deep into their surroundings and this hike is one of the best in Rocky for sensing the power of water to carve the landscape.

At about a mile-and-a-half from the ranger station you arrive at one of the landmarks on this trail, a log bridge across the roaring creek. Stop here for a drink of water (not from the creek, though) and to get a good long look at the creek itself. It bounces across rocks, eddies into little pools and flows gracefully around curves and bends.

You've been going gradually uphill, but now you begin some real work. The last third-mile or so of this hike climbs steadily through the thick, dense woods of a subalpine forest. With so little light reaching the ground, don't expect to see a lot of wildflowers. Instead, watch for the many small mammals you're likely to find—squirrels and chipmunks.

When you reach the dead-end intersection turn right and within a few steps you've reached Calypso Cascades.

In late spring and early summer look around among the rocks for the Calypso orchids which give these falls their name.

More!
Follow Hike Three to Ouzel Falls.

Day hikers walk to Ouzel Falls

~ 3 ~ Ouzel Falls

Fast Facts

A variety of ecosystems and the best views of Wild Basin. This trail passes through a fire-damaged area, which provides insight into the way forests repair themselves.

Length: 2.7 miles each way
Elevation Change: 950 feet
Map on Page: 14
Designation: Easy Hike
Amenities: Ranger station, restrooms, wheelchair accessible
Trailhead: Wild Basin Ranger Station: On Colorado Highway 7, south of Estes Park approximately 13 miles, take the Wild Basin turn off into the park. Pass through the entrance station and follow the road approximately 2 miles to the ranger station.

Enjoy your hike past Copeland Falls and Calypso Cascades. This trail edges along North St. Vrain and Cony Creeks. The geology along the creek is interesting as well, telling a veritable history of glaciers carving valleys and piling up moraines, and then creeks tearing it all down.

As you approach the end of the Calypso Cascades trail look on your left for a Park Service sign describing the causes and effects of fire. The Calypso Cascades trail dead ends into the Allen's Park and Finch Lake trail. Follow the well-marked directions to turn right, west, toward Ouzel Falls.

Immediately you know you've come out of the creek's influence. As you leave the south side of Cony Creek's valley the dark forest gives way to sprightlier aspen.

This stretch of hike feels wide-open is because a fire ravaged these parts in 1978. Lightning caused this conflagration which burned 1,050 acres.

Though fires seem dangerous and devastating they cleanse an area and begin the forest-growth cycle anew. Expect to see tall, bark-stripped lodgepole pine accenting broad stretches of mountain side lush with wildflowers, bushes and saplings.

After the trail switches up a couple hundred feet of elevation, you arrive at the goal, Ouzel Falls. Look for its namesake—the ouzel—cavorting among the sprays. These brown birds are also known as dippers.

Moss on the roots of a tree

A fir's gentle needles

~ 4 ~ Eugenia Mine

Fast Facts

This is the perfect stroll along an easy path for those times when you want to get away from it all.

Length: 1.4 miles each way
Elevation Change: 500 feet
Map on Page: 20
Designation: Easy Hike
Amenities: Ranger station, restrooms, wheelchair accessible
Trailhead: Longs Peak Trailhead: From Colorado Highway 7, south of Estes Park about nine miles, turn into the Longs Peak Ranger Station and Campground. Drive approximately one mile to the large parking lot. Longs Peak is one of the most popular hikes in the state so this lot is likely to be crowded. Arrive early in the day or later in the afternoon.

The trail begins just to the left of the ranger station. Right from the start this trail, wide and well maintained, begins to gradually climb. About one-half-mile along the trail, take a right onto the marked trail to Eugenia Mine and Estes Cone.

To reach the mine you'll stroll, ever higher, for 0.9 miles. The trail travels mostly through lodgepole pine with only patches of quaking aspen. Early or late it's shady and cool, but may be hot in the middle of the day. Eventually, after loosing yourself in thought many times over, you cross Inn Brook over a pair of downed and trimmed logs and arrive at the mine site.

It's amazing to think that people actually lived and worked in what we now know as a national park. Carl Norwall built the cabin here around the turn of the century. It was quite comfortable apparently, but the mine he dug didn't pay out. The site was abandoned around 1920.

Be sure to follow up the creek a few yards to see tailings and ruined mining machinery.

More!

Walk along the trail toward Estes Cone as far as you like.

Lily Mountain and Lily Lake

~ 5 ~ Lily Lake Loop

This trail has asphalt or boardwalk paving for its entire half-mile circuit around Lily Lake. If you take the walk clockwise you'll head out of the parking lot bearing left and pass some trees before you head into a marshy area of swaying grass. Many mountain lakes eventually fill up with the soil being deposited by the creeks that feed them. These marsh grasses are evidence that this lake is indeed soiling up. Moving around, you pass through an area of ponderosa pine on the far edge of the lake. A wide gravel road invites exploration here. Then the trail snuggles right along the base of Lily Mountain before curling its way back to the parking lot.

Begin or finish this walk with a visit to the log structure housing a visitor center on the eastern side of Colorado High-

way 7. The center has modern displays highlighting many aspects of the park and nearby national forest. Helpful staff answer questions and if they're not busy they share their own hiking experiences in the area. A book store offers a wide selection of informative materials, plus they nearly always have a video running and a fire burning.

Be very cautious when crossing Colorado Highway 7 in either direction. Traffic can be quite heavy and blind curves and the nearby entrance to a bed and breakfast inn make this a risky stretch of road.

Autumn color near the East Portal Trail

~ 6 ~ East Portal/YMCA

Fast Facts

Loop Emerald Mountain with views of the Wind River Valley and Hallett Peak.

Length: 6 mile loop
Elevation Change: 300 feet
Map on Page: 20
Designation: Easy Hike
Amenities: Restrooms, restaurant and gift shop at YMCA
Trailhead: East Portal Parking Lot: Follow US Highway 36 west out of Estes Park to the YMCA turnoff (also known as County Highway 66). Follow this for approximately 3.5 miles, passing the YMCA turnoff, to the parking lot at the dead-end of this highway near a commercial campground. Do not drive past the campground to the dam, no parking is available there.

Find the trail on the north side of the road heading left, or west, toward the mountain you see in front of you. That is Emerald Mountain. You can see the trail snaking up its flank. All the elevation gain for this hike is in this first half-mile. Enjoy walking through this Montane ecosystem of ponderosa pine and sage. Be sure to turn back to enjoy the views of the mountains. The lake you pass is human-made from water shunted through the mountains via tunnel.

You arrive at a T-intersection where the horse trail from the YMCA passes. Bear left. The trail climbs then levels off into an aspen glen. You are at 8,600 feet above sea level. Take time to explore this area. As you cross this saddle northward you enter Glacier Basin.

The trail dead ends into the long Glacier Basin Trail. For a rewarding vista turn left and progress for a half-mile or so to catch Hallett Peak. But to follow this loop trail, turn right onto the Glacier Basin Trail. The sign is clearly marked for the YMCA. Now the trail leads gradually downward, through dense forest toward the YMCA. Keep an eye open for horse droppings. Where the trail splits, one arm heading right and up, and the other heading left, take the left.

The trail gradually leads you into the YMCA camp. Follow the dirt road past the stables. Go along the road toward the camp entrance. A track to the right parallels the road 1.5 miles back to the trailhead.

4

Eugenia Mine

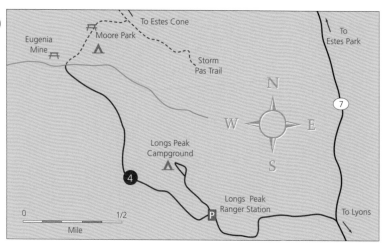

5

Lily Lake

6

East Portal/ YMCA

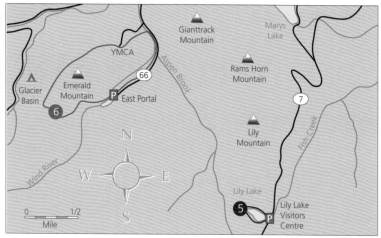

7

Moraine Park Museum

10

Big Thompson River

Moraine Park Museum

~ 7 ~ Moraine Park Museum

Length: 0.65 mile loop
Elevation Change: 45 feet
Map on Page: 20
Designation: Walk
Amenities: Restrooms and bookstore at Moraine Park Museum
Trailhead: Moraine Park Museum: Take US Highway 36 west out of Estes Park, past the park headquarters and into Rocky via the Beaver Meadows entrance station. Drive on 0.2 miles and take a left onto the Bear Lake Road. Drive approximately 1 mile to the Moraine Park Museum on the left.

This gravel trail winds through a ponderosa pine forest behind the Moraine Park Museum. Begin near the front entrance and follow the gravel trail as it loops into the trees, behind and above the museum and coming back out near the parking lot.

Notice markers along the trail, indicating the species of the various flowers, bushes and trees common to this ecosystem. This is a classic south-facing montane system sprinkled with red-barked ponderosa pine, many wildflowers and dry grasses. From the trail behind the museum study the geology of the area a bit. The ridges to the right and left are lateral moraines, which are huge rock deposits left by the glaciers that carved Moraine Park. As this valley (or "park") heads up into the mountains you can detect the "U"-shape which glaciers carve.

The lateral moraine to the left is a classic north-facing montane system, characterized with dense forest of lodgepole pine and Douglas fir.

Benches invite walkers to rest for a minute and take in the vistas up Moraine Park and Longs Peak.

The museum itself has plenty to offer. Displays explain how these immense valleys were formed during various periods of glaciation. For a rest, head into the sitting area on the second floor, it has one of the best up-valley views in Rocky.

The Pool

The Ferns

~ 8 ~ The Pool and Fern Falls

Fast Facts

Streams edge, massive rocks, dramatic pool, misty falls

Length: 1.7 each way to The Pool, add 1 mile to Fern Falls
Elevation Change: 250 feet to The Pool, add 400 to Fern Falls
Map on Page: 24
Designation: Hike
Amenities: Restrooms at Fern Lake Trailhead
Trailhead: Enter the park at Beaver Meadows entrance station, turn south (left) onto Bear Lake Road. At 1.2 miles turn west (right) onto the gravel road for the Moraine Park Campground. After 0.7 miles or so take a left onto the gravel road which drops down to the left. Take this road past the Cub Lake Trailhead to where it dead ends at the Fern Lake Trailhead.

This is one of the classic easy hikes of Rocky Mountain National Park. The trail follows the Big Thompson River for quite a while, coursing through willow and alder bushes. The river is clear and inviting. Look for beaver dams and stop and dawdle along the sandy beaches which edge the river.

After about a mile the trail winds its way into a bizarre clump of rocks. They seem so out of place, far away from any mountain and near the river, they could only have been heaved here by a glacier thousands of years ago. Kids love playing among the boulders and indeed they offer many opportunities for creativity.

The trail begins to climb more steadily, above the river and along the side of Beaver Mountain as it turns the corner up into Forest Canyon.

You are hiking uphill among striking aspen glens. After a quarter mile or so you reach The Pool. Here, while the river is squeezed between massive boulders, it found a place to spread out and relax a bit. The bridge offers a good view but follow the trail up a bit for an even better vista.

Now the trail ascends uphill rapidly through subalpine forest to the 40-foot drop of misty Fern Falls.

More!

Follow the trail to Cub Lake. This adds about three miles distance and another 400 feet elevation to this hike, climbing a ridge before the trail drops to edge its way along lily-covered Cub Lake.

Cub Lake

~ 9 ~ Cub Lake

Fast Facts

Passing through beautiful scenery and many ecosystems this hike finishes with vistas of lily-choked Cub Lake

Length: 2.3 miles each way
Elevation Change: 540 feet
Map on Page: 24
Designation: Hike
Amenities: Water at Cub Lake Trailhead, portable toilets
Trailhead: Cub Lake Trailhead: Enter the park at Beaver Meadows Entrance Station, turn south (left) onto Bear Lake Road. At 1.2 miles turn west (right) onto the gravel road for the Moraine Park Campground. After 0.7 miles or so take a left onto the gravel road which drops down to the left. Take this road to the Cub Lake Trailhead. Lot fills early.

This is one of the most scenic and rewarding of the easier hikes in Rocky. And with good reason; it passes through jaw-dropping scenery on its way to a lovely lake ringed with gnarly mountains.

The trail begins with a series of bridges spanning splashing creeks and the Big Thompson River itself. This moist area is likely to be abloom with cow parsnip and other water-needy plants.

Eventually the gravel trail traces its way through beautiful stands of ponderosa pine scattered with immense boulders carried here by glaciers.

Now we begin the uphill portion of the hike. The walkway wanders through aspen stands flanked by wildflower-strewn meadows.

Keep an eye out for wildlife too. Hike early in the cool of the early morning and you are likely to see deer, rabbits and even a partridge or two.

After a series of switchbacks the trail levels off and finds its way through the forest into the openness surrounding Cub Lake. This lake is aflutter with yellow-blossomed pond lilies and framed with steep ridges backed with massive mountains.

This hike passes through several ecosystems: riparian, wet and dry montane and sub-alpine forest.

More!

At Cub Lake follow the trail to Fern Falls, The Pool, and back to the trailhead, making this a loop hike and adding 3.7 miles.

8
The Pool/ Fern Falls

9
Cub Lake

[Map showing trails to The Pool, Fern Falls, Cub Lake with markers for Arch Rocks, Big Thompson River, Fern Lake Trailhead, Cub Lake Trailhead, Moraine Park Campgrounds, To Bear Lake Road, Moraine Park, Ponds, Steep Mountain, and a compass rose. Scale 0 to 1/2 Mile.]

Moraine Park Campgrounds
To Bear Lake Road
Fern Lake Trailhead
Arch Rocks
Cub Lake Trailhead
The Pool
Big Thompson River
Moraine Park
To Fern Falls
Cub Lake
Ponds
Steep Mountain
0   1/2
Mile

N W E S

Enos Mills

While the efforts of many people contributed to the formation of Rocky Mountain National Park, Enos Mills is remembered as its most ardent supporter.

Mills first came to the area in 1884 at the age of 14. By 1890, he had claimed a homestead at the foot of Longs Peak. From his tiny cabin he supported himself as a professional guide and naturalist. In 1902 he purchased the Longs Peak Inn where guests availed themselves of his expert mountaineering services.

In time, Mills and other long-time residents of the area could see the toll that development was taking on the glacial moraines and alpine highlands they loved. Although the area was now largely contained within the Medicine Bow Forest Reserve, the designation did little to secure the fragile environment. Mills wholeheartedly endorsed suggestions to make the territory a "wildlife preserve," advocating that it

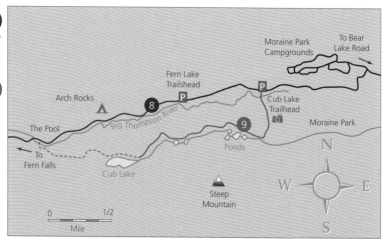

should include more than 1,000 square miles and stretch from Estes Park to Colorado Springs.

President Theodore Roosevelt backed Mills and commissioned him to undertake cross-country lectures to promote the land's preservation. Mills proved to be an excellent speaker and an effective naturalist writer, penning articles for the *Saturday Evening Post, Harper's,* and *Atlantic,* in addition to several books.

The campaign paid off in 1915 when Congress and President Woodrow Wilson created Rocky Mountain National Park, the nation's tenth such national preserve.

It was less than half the size originally proposed by Mills. But at least it now had become a sanctuary for future generations, a place to "put one in tune with the infinite," as Mills wrote.

The Big Thompson River flowing through Moraine Park

~ 10 ~ Big Thompson River

Simply park the car, pack up the backpack, grab the kids and head for the bridge you see spanning the Big Thompson river. Instead of crossing it though look for the trail heading into the grasses along river's edge. This hike is easy—simply follow this footpath among the grasses as far as your heart carries you, then turn around and come back.

You're walking through riparian habitat, lush with grass, birds and the occasional bug. The forest-covered ridge to the left is a lateral moraine; a ridge of rock left by the glacier. Ahead string out the mountains of the Front Range.

The river loops along leaving beaches of gravel to play or picnic on. Look for trout scurrying around in the pools. Fisherfolk enjoy this area because of its easy access to the water.

To your left, you can see the majesty of Longs Peak, ahead lies Forest Canyon reaching into the deepest, highest regions of Rocky Mountain National Park.

These wide, river bottoms are often called "parks." This park was once dotted with cabins and a resort hotel. At one time a golf course made its way through.

The cabins you see to the south are called "in-holdings." They have been there since before the park was founded in 1915.

Aspen trees in late sun

Douglas fir

~ 11 ~ Mill Creek Basin

Fast Facts

A wide, sagebrush-lined roadway leads to aspen grooves and beaver ponds. An uphill climb through dark forest works up to a lush alpine meadow perfect for picnicking.

Length: 1.6 miles each way
Elevation Change: 600 feet
Map on Page: 32
Designation: Hike
Amenities: Restrooms
Trailhead: Hollowell Park Trailhead.: Take US Highway 36 into Rocky via the Beaver Meadows Entrance Station. Drive on 0.2 mile and take the left turn onto the Bear Lake Road. Drive approximately 3.5 miles south until you reach the right turn (west) onto the gravel road for the Hallowell Park Trailhead.

The first third of this hike roams along a dusty road. It's an excellent stretch for getting used to the altitude. Here you sense the wide open Colorado sky all around, you can smell the pine and hear the birds calling. The middle third works through the aspen groves that line Mill Creek. Beaver workings are evident. The final third is a real climb through deep forest till you reach a big, flower-strewn meadow, open to the big sky above.

This is a great trail for finding peace and quiet. While the trail is well tended and easy, it is little frequented—a lovely sunrise or sunset hike.

Watch for deer in the first third of this hike, birds in the second and squirrels in the third.

Shuttle Parking Lot

To relieve the congestion at Bear Lake, a parking lot has been constructed among the trees across Bear Lake Road from Glacier Basin Campground. Large, free shuttle buses make passenger pick-ups every half-hour or less in a loop that includes the parking lot itself, the Bierstadt Lake trailhead, Glacier Gorge Junction and Bear Lake.

From Bierstadt Lake catch a glimpse of a glacial bowl

~ 12 ~ Bierstadt Lake Hike

Fast Facts

Stunning views of glacial valleys and mountain peaks, pretty alpine lake

Length: 2.3 mile hike plus shuttle return to car
Elevation Change: 550 feet
Map on Page: 32
Designation: Hike
Amenities: Ranger station, restrooms, wheelchair accessible
Trailhead: Bear Lake shuttle parking lot: Enter Rocky via the Beaver Meadows entrance station. Drive on 0.2 mile and take the left turn onto the Bear Lake Road. Head south 5.1 miles to the well-marked Bear Lake shuttle parking lot.

If you park in the shuttle parking lot and begin hiking there, you will be strolling downhill during the most scenic part of this walk and then simply hop the shuttle back to your car.

Park at the lot and look for the trail heading up the embankment at the far end of the parking lot. The trail climbs through dense forest of lodgepole pine. This steady climb is the preferred way to gain the elevation in this hike. After a mile you begin to glimpse the lake off to the right.

A short stroll around Bierstadt reveals many quiet nooks among the trees and rocks to stop for some quiet time or a picnic. Go around the lake—its edge is marshy— far enough to spot Longs Peak reflected in the water.

Follow the signs for Bierstadt Lake Trailhead. This will lead deep into the woods and suddenly break free onto the top of Bierstadt Moraine. The trail switchbacks its way down the edge of the moraine, alternating up-valley and down-valley vistas. You actually finish at the Bierstadt Lake Trailhead, but if you had started here you would have been slogging up those switchbacks—quite possibly exhausted and sunburned— rather than casually descending and enjoying the scenery.

Carefully cross Bear Lake Road to take a north-bound shuttle back to the shuttle parking lot.

More!
From Bierstadt Lake take the trail on to Bear Lake.

This view from Sprague Lake is perhaps the most-photographed view of Hallett Peak

~ 13 ~ Sprague Lake Loop

Park in the large parking lot and head for the bridge across Glacier Creek. This sparkling water course is a lively stress reducer. The paved trail around the lake begins within a few yards. Take your time, looking for ducks on the water and squirrels among the trees. You might also see Clark's nutcrackers and lively Steller's jays. Several platforms built out near the water take advantage of wonderful views. Information markers provide a lot of interesting facts about the history of settlement in this area.

Halfway around the lake, large boulders and benches invite you to rest. Have a drink of water and enjoy the mountain vistas. The slope-topped mountain is Hallett Peak, 12,713 feet above sea level. Its neighbor is Flattop Mountain, a mere 12,324 feet.

Abner Sprague was a homesteader. He first settled in Moraine Park up the road but moved here to start a fishing preserve at the lake. Even today you're likely to see fishers out in the water in their hip boots.

Horses are stabled at Sprague Lake. This is an excellent opportunity to go for a guided horseback ride.

More!

The Sprague Lake area has much to offer adventurous day-hikers. Simply pack the essentials and begin walking. Many of the hikes will add considerable distance and elevation.

Squirrel

Alberta Falls

~ 14 ~ Alberta Falls

Fast Facts

Very scenic walk with long, valley and waterfall vistas

Length: 0.6 miles each way
Elevation Change: 160 feet
Map on Page: 32
Designation: Easy hike
Amenities: Restrooms
Trailhead: Glacier Gorge Junction Trailhead: Take US 36 west out of Estes Park. Enter the park at Beaver Meadows entrance station, turn south (left) onto Bear Lake Road. Drive 8.5 miles to Glacier Gorge Trailhead parking lot. This is a very small parking lot so it may be wiser to park at the shuttle parking lot (5.1 miles south of US 36) and take the shuttle bus to the Glacier Creek drop off.

This is one of the most scenic easy hikes in Rocky Mountain National Park. The trail begins on the east side of the road. Be careful crossing the highway. The walk starts with a little downhill stretch. At the trail crossing, follow the signs for Alberta Falls. Immediately the trail heads through aspen glens and pine forests. It dips down to cross lively streams several times. Avoid the temptation to drink the water.

Leading through colorful and lively aspen groves, this is an excellent stroll for fall color. In summer, look for wildflowers; red paintbrush or Colorado columbine. It's very likely that you'll see squirrels scurrying around, hoarding nuts for the winter. And birds are sure to pass by.

The trail begins to climb in about a quarter of a mile, working its way up the side of a moraine.

You begin to hear the water itself when all of a sudden the trail turns a switchback. Immediately you are overlooking all of Glacier Gorge. Ahead is Bierstadt Moraine. To see the misty, exhilarating falls you walk another 100 yards and scramble—very carefully—onto the pinkish red rocks.

These falls are one of the wonders of Rocky. They dash from rock to rock in a sprightly display of snowy runoff.

More!

Take the trail on up to Mills Lake (Hike 15), one of the best hikes in the park, adding about 2 miles each way and 500 feet of elevation.

Mills Lake in morning light

~ 15 ~ Mills Lake

Fast Facts

Among the most scenic hikes in the park, a lovely trail leads through many environments to a stunning alpine lake reflecting Longs Peak itself.

Length: 2.5 miles each way
Elevation Change: 700 feet
Map on Page: 32
Designation: Hike
Amenities: Restrooms
Trailhead: Glacier Gorge: Enter the park at Beaver Meadows entrance station, turn south (left) onto Bear Lake Road. Drive 8.5 miles to Glacier Gorge Trailhead parking lot. This is a very small parking lot so it may be wiser to park at the shuttle parking lot (5.1 miles south of US 36) and take the shuttle bus to the Glacier Creek drop off.

Carefully cross the road and follow the signs toward Alberta Falls. This is a lovely trail leading through aspen glens and offering wide vistas of Glacier Gorge. The falls themselves are a great spot to stop for water and a snack.

Returning to the trail after exploring, head uphill. The trail here is quite rocky. It passes up several switchbacks providing fantastic views. West you glimpse Hallett Peak and Flattop Mountain.

Eventually the trail reaches a high point and you bank around the flank of Glacier Knob. The mountain to your left as the trail gradually descends is Half Mountain but you see Thatchtop, McHenrys and Longs Peak as well.

The trail descends into a forest. At an intersection follow the signs for Mills Lake.

Eventually the trail seems to fade out among huge rocks on the ground. It's there, you just have to follow it in a different way across the rocks. Look for small, human-made piles of rocks. These are called "cairns" and they guide you across broad rocky areas.

The trail breaks out into wide open vistas. Mills Lake snuggles up to the steep drop-offs of Thatchtop Mountain (12,668). But the peak that really draws your eye is Longs Peak itself.

More!

Add 2.2 miles each way and another 700 feet of gain to reach alpine Black Lake. Take warm clothes and rain gear.

Left: A wind-blown tree frames Mills Lake

11 Mill Creek Basin

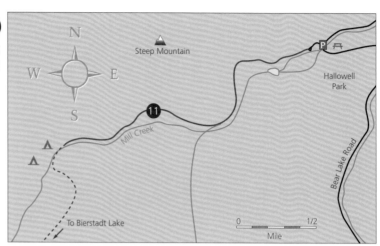

12 Bierstadt Lake

13 Sprague Lake Walk

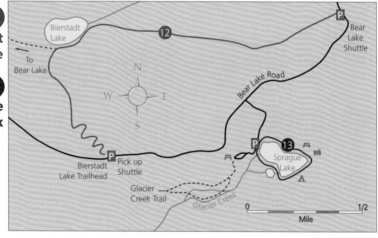

14 Alberta Falls

15 Mills Lake

16 The Loch

Wildflowers on the trail   *A Colorado columbine*

~ 16 ~ The Loch

Fast Facts

Wide open scenery through many geological and environmental features ends in a perfect alpine lake surrounded by mountains.

Length: 2.7 miles each way
Elevation Change: 970 feet
Map on Page: 32
Designation: Hike
Amenities: Restrooms
Trailhead: Wild Basin Ranger Station: Enter the park at Beaver Meadows entrance station, turn south (left) onto Bear Lake Road. Drive 8.5 miles to Glacier Gorge Trailhead parking lot. This is a very small parking lot so it may be wiser to park at the shuttle parking lot (5.1 miles south of US 36) and take the shuttle bus to the Glacier Creek drop off.

Enjoy the scenery, wildflowers and wildlife as if you were on your way to Mills Lake. At approximately 2.0 miles, in a forested area, you come to a sign guiding you to The Loch. Then the trail climbs rigorous switchbacks until you reach The Loch.

The view is your reward. Taylor and Powell Peaks dominate the vista. Cathedral Wall rises along the southeast shore.

This hike is among the more popular hikes in the park offering a good workout balanced with exciting scenery.

Every week during the summer, rangers guide interested hikers up to The Loch. Check at any ranger station for details.

Looking south across Bear Lake

~ 17 ~ Bear Lake Nature Trail

With good reason the Bear Lake Nature Trail is one of the most popular circuits in the state.

Simply pass the ranger information station, head into the woods on the paved trail and before you can say Clark's nutcracker you're in the wilderness following this accessible trail past some of Colorado's grandest vistas.

As you arrive you see Hallett Peak poking its head into the (usually) big blue sky. Progressing around you discern Longs Peak and the Keyboard of the Winds. Glacier Gorge carves its way right toward Estes Park, and from the lake's south edge you can spy Flattop and Notchtop Mountains.

You're very likely to see wildlife. Clark's nutcrackers and Steller's jays are common as are golden-mantled ground squirrels and chipmunks. You just might see one or two greenback cutthroat trout, reintroduced several years ago and thriving. Aspen, Engelmann spruce, subalpine fir and lodgepole pine—so named because Native Americans used them to build tipi lodges—are common.

More!
Any number of hikes take off from Bear Lake. Nymph Lake leading to Dream Lake and Emerald Lake are popular. The hike down to Alberta Falls is also rewarding; you can hike down to the Glacier Gorge Trailhead then up to the falls.

Nymph Lake and Hallett Peak

~ 18 ~ Nymph Lake

Fast Facts

An easy climb through a forest takes hikers to a lily-filled lake at the base of Hallett Peak.

Length: 0.5 miles each way
Elevation Change: 225 feet
Map on Page: 39
Designation: Easy hike
Amenities: Ranger station, restrooms, shuttle service, water
Trailhead: Bear Lake Trailhead: Enter the park at Beaver Meadows entrance station, after about 0.2 miles turn south (left) onto Bear Lake Road. Go south 9 miles to the end of the road. This parking lot fills up early in the day so it may be wiser to park at the shuttle parking lot which is 5.1 miles south of US 36 and take the shuttle bus to Bear Lake.

Head past the ranger station and cross the bridge. Soon you arrive at signage guiding you to Nymph, Dream and Emerald lakes. Follow the trail to Nymph Lake. The trail climbs slowly through subalpine forest around the shoulder of the glacial moraine which traps both Bear and Nymph lakes. The path is wide and paved.

You arrive on the southeast corner of Nymph Lake. The trail continues around the lake but many side spurs invite you down to water's edge. As the trail passes the lake's northern side, log benches and huge boulders offer convenient places to sit and contemplate the reflection of Hallett Peak in the waters of Nymph Lake. This is one of the most photogenic views in Rocky.

You might think this lake should be named "lily-pad lake" for it is thriving with these water loving plants. In fact, this species once had the Latin name *Nymphaea polysepal*a. The name stuck—to the lake at least, the plant species name was revised decades ago. Bright yellow flowers catch the eye from early July through August.

More!

Head on up to Dream (Hike Nineteen) and Emerald Lake (Hike 20) or Lake Haiyaha (Hike Twenty One).

Dream Lake

~ 19 ~ Dream Lake

Fast Facts

This elegantly long lake reflects Hallett Peak. The trail offers an uphill stretch but rewards with great scenery.

Length: 1.1 miles each way
Elevation Change: 425 feet
Map on Page: 39
Designation: Hike
Amenities: Ranger station, restrooms, shuttle service, water
Trailhead: Bear Lake Trailhead: Enter the park at Beaver Meadows entrance station, after about 0.2 miles turn south (left) onto Bear Lake Road. Go south 9 miles to the end of the road. This parking lot fills up early in the day so it may be wiser to park at the shuttle parking lot which is 5.1 miles south of US 36 and take the shuttle bus to Bear Lake.

Head past the ranger station and cross the bridge. Soon you arrive at signage guiding you to Nymph, Dream and Emerald lakes. Take the trail to Nymph Lake.

The trail to Dream Lake loops around Nymph Lake. At the north end of Nymph, the trail rises around a couple of switchbacks. Take your time up this trail, particularly if you've just arrived in the park from lower elevations. Going slow has real rewards too, because you can pause to enjoy the wide open views the trail frames. Look below to admire Nymph Lake from above. Across one stretch you can see Bear Lake nestled into its geology of glacial deposits.

Eventually you reach a marker guiding you to bear right across a bridge to Dream Lake. A rock outcropping just across the stream is a great place to frame up photographs and pause for a drink of water. The trail heads on up the valley, but side trails lead down to Dream Lake.

It would be too easy to say that this lake, surrounded by rugged mountains and rocks and meadows adrift in wildflowers, is a dream come true.

More!
Point your boots toward Emerald Lake (Hike 20) or Lake Haiyaha (Hike 21).

The trail to Emerald Lake

Emerald Lake

~ 20 ~ Emerald Lake

Fast Facts

A rugged hike finishes with this lake surrounded by magnificent cliffs and cirques.

Length: 1.8 miles each way
Elevation Change: 605 feet
Map on Page: 39
Designation: Hike
Amenities: Ranger station, restrooms, shuttle service, water
Trailhead: Bear Lake Trailhead: Enter the park at Beaver Meadows entrance station, after about 0.2 miles turn south (left) onto Bear Lake Road. Go south 9 miles to the end of the road. This parking lot fills up early in the day so it may be wiser to park at the shuttle parking lot which is 5.1 miles south of US 36 and take the shuttle bus to Bear Lake.

Head past the ranger station and cross the bridge. Soon you arrive at signage guiding you to Nymph, Dream and Emerald Lakes. Take the trail to Nymph Lake. It loops around and climbs toward Dream Lake. At the trails intersection to Lake Haiyaha bear right and head across the stream to Dream Lake. As you pass Dream Lake bear right around the lake.

The trail to Emerald begins to climb right away. Though a popular trail, this is real backcountry hiking. You must scramble over rocks and work your way over house-sized boulders and alongside a waterfall of Tyndall Creek as this trail rises through forest and eventually to the glacially-formed cirque which holds Emerald Lake.

Find a spot on the rocks to sit and admire this bowl. After a while you notice two small waterfalls revealing themselves along the immense rock spillways. To the left rises Hallett Peak, though here, at last, you get a different view of this Rocky mainstay. To the right Flattop rears up, though it seems anything but flat from this view.

The water of Emerald Lake is often green from glacial runoff.

More!
Work your way around Emerald Lake on the rocks. But be careful, it's easy to fall.

Extensive rockfall near Haiyaha

It's hard to get lost in Rocky

~ 21 ~ Lake Haiyaha

Head past the ranger station and cross the bridge. Soon you arrive at signage guiding you to Nymph, Dream and Emerald Lakes. Take the trail to Nymph Lake. After reaching Nymph it loops around and climbs toward Dream Lake. At the intersection to Lake Haiyaha follow the arrow and head up the hill and into the woods.

The trail climbs rather steeply up into a dark alpine forest. After several switchbacks it opens up into truly breath-stopping views of Bear and Nymph Lakes as well as Longs Peak and the valleys leading up to it. This is an excellent place to stop and have a drink of water and a snack.

Then the way descends a bit back into forest before opening out among gigantic boulders. Continue across these until you reach the lake's edge.

Be very careful here as it is easy to slip and fall or turn an ankle. However, these home-size granitics offer some fun opportunities for a picnic in the sunshine.

In fact, this high alpine watering hole is surrounded by these immense rocks. They even give the lake its name—Haiyaha—which means "Big Rocks."

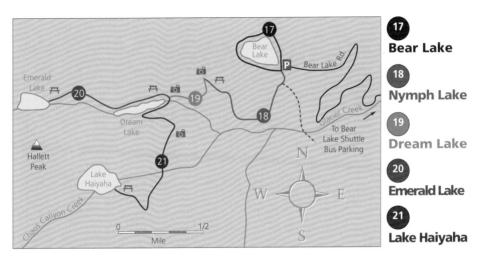

17 Bear Lake

18 Nymph Lake

19 Dream Lake

20 Emerald Lake

21 Lake Haiyaha

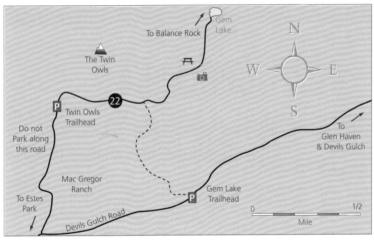

22 Gem Lake

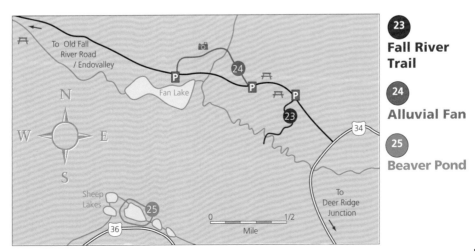

23 Fall River Trail

24 Alluvial Fan

25 Beaver Pond

39

Twin Owls formation on the trail to Gem Lake

~ 22 ~ Gem Lake

This is the steepest hike described in this book. But the scenery along the way makes it worth every panting breath. Begin early in the morning to avoid the heat of the sun which hammers these south-facing slopes.

The trail begins in a cool, forested grove, climbing along the flanks of Lumpy Ridge. You won't hike far before you realize why the area is called lumpy. The rock formations look like mounds of potato mashings. The views up to the ridges or back toward Estes Park are exceptional. Take your time and drink plenty of water. Eventually the trail winds its way across massive slabs of granite and climbs steeply into a narrow canyon. A series of tight switchbacks swerve ever upward. Will it never end? Yes, and when it does you'll be at Gem Lake.

As jeweled lakes in Rocky go, this is a tiny gem at best. It sets in a steep, pink-stone rock-bowl formation seem-ingly dammed with trees. Be sure to hike around to the far side. Climb up the rocks there to one of the several shelves and you can see back across the lake all the way to Longs Peak. A small beach-like area invites picnickers to spread out and dip their hike-heated toes into the water.

As you return, it's downhill all the way and as you savor the views you realize that, with this hike in particular, the fun is as much in the journey as the destination.

Why don't we take this Gem Lake hike from the Gem

The Rocks of Rocky

Paul Bunyon's Boot

With the millions of tons of rocks laying around the area, it's probably no coincidence that this park is nicknamed Rocky.

Most of the rocks hereabout are of three types: gneiss, schist and granite.

Narrow bands of dark minerals streaking across a rock face are the sign of schist. Wider stripes and lighter colors are a clue that you are looking at gneiss.

These are both metamorphic rocks, formed when layers of sediment are altered from mere sedimentary rocks by pressure and/or movement deep within the earth.

The third type is granite. Granites are the pinkish or gray stones you see. With granites you see flecks of minerals, not lines or striations.

Lake trailhead? You can. Simply follow Highway 43 around that bend, and in another mile or so turn left into the Gem Lake trailhead. Hiking from here adds elevation and distance to an already steep hike though and the first half-mile isn't nearly as pretty as the first half-mile from the Twin Owls trailhead.

Glaciers

Glaciers are enormous masses of frozen water. They build up after decades of cold weather and hundreds of feet of snowfall slowly crushes itself into ice by its own weight. Glaciers are incredibly heavy, yet they do actually flow.

Over years of successive freezing and thawing, they travel forward or backward as snow accumulates or melts. Because of this motion they tear up the ground all around them. They develop in "V"-shaped valleys, but when they are finished scraping along, they have torn the valley into a distinctive "U"-shape. They also push enormous quantities of material out in front of their path, called terminal moraines, and along the sides, called lateral moraines. Their distinctive touch is clearly seen throughout the park's rounded valley walls, bowl-shaped basins and "park" meadows.

Arete
Narrow jagged spine topping a series of cirques. Look for the Keyboard of the Winds formation running up to Longs Peak.

Cirque
Steep-walled, semicircular basins, or bowls, appearing at the top of high, glacially-carved valleys. This is where a glacier actually begins. Most notably in Rocky notice the immense bowl cirque behind the Alpine Visitor Center.

Erratics
Huge boulders, once embedded in the flowing ice of the glacier, but left behind when the glacier retreated.

Hanging Valley
"U"-shaped hanging valleys are smaller glaciers which flow into larger ones, forming a valley high on the wall of a larger valley. Look for these as you travel up Trail Ridge Road.

Lateral Moraine
Long ridges of debris and soil pushed to the sides of a glacier as it flows. These are the large ridges you see as you drive Bear Lake Road. To walk on one take the Bierstadt Lake hike.

Terminal Moraine
Headwalls of debris pushed into place by the toe of a glacier. Moraine Park Museum is built on a terminal moraine.

Tarn
A small, high mountain lake formed in the path of a glacier. Emerald Lake is one such and you can see many of these across the valley from Forest Canyon Overlook.

Horn
A pyramidal peak formed by the intersection of several cirques. Check out Longs Peak.

Thistle choke out other species

Fall River

~ 23 ~ Fall River Trail

Fast Facts

A serene stroll on the banks of Fall River

Length: 0.5–2 miles
Elevation Change: 20 feet
Map on Page: 39
Designation: Walk
Amenities: None
Trailhead: Parking lot between Lawn Lake Trailhead and Alluvial Fan parking lot: come west out of Estes Park on US Highway 34, enter the park at the Fall River entrance station, then drive 2.1 miles to the Endovalley turnoff. Head up valley. Pass the Lawn Lake trailhead. Keep an eye open toward the left for a parking lot for several cars.

The trail, such as it is, leads out of the left-hand corner of the parking lot. It crosses a grass-covered knob rising to the highest point on this easy stroll. Soon it drops to the overgrown banks of the river. Follow any of the little trails which present themselves to get to the stream's edge or simply stroll along the footpath, occasionally hopping across small creeks, to enjoy the setting.

You are in the riparian habitat along Fall River in the heart of Horseshoe Park. As you look across the river you can see Trail Ridge Road snaking up Beaver Mountain toward Hidden Valley. Looking to the right you can see the rugged Mummy Range, the definitive string of peaks in this corner of Rocky.

Come here in the autumn and the chances are good you'll spot elk in the vicinity.

More!
Continue walking and exploring this lush riparian habitat..

The waterfall created by the Lawn Lake flood dwarfs human beings

~ 24 ~ Alluvial Fan Trail

Fast Facts

See the force of water at work and a high waterfall

Length: 0.5 miles each way
Elevation Change: 50 feet
Map on Page: 39
Designation: Walk
Amenities: Restrooms, wheelchair accessible
Trailhead: Alluvial Fan Trail parking lot: Come west out of Estes Park on US Highway 34. Enter the park at the Fall River entrance station, then drive 2.1 miles to the Endovalley turnoff. From the Endovalley turnoff head up valley. The parking lot for Alluvial Fan Trail is on your right about 0.5 miles along Endovalley.

This paved trail leads from the parking lot into a bit of forest and out onto the rock debris left by the Lawn Lake flood. The trail crawls up to an overlook and drops down to another parking lot on the other side. Along the way it crosses a stream which is a popular waterway for parents and their kids to explore one of Rocky's wetter features.

From the lookout check out the nearby features. The lake you see near the road was formed when debris from the flood blocked Fall River's course. Hundreds of trees and other plants were killed and carried away.

No one really stays on the trail for long. Almost everyone who comes by to see the debris fan ends up scrambling up the rocks. Be careful, they can twist your ankle.

Lawn Lake Flood

In the early morning hours of July 15, 1982, the earth dam at Lawn Lake burst about four miles north of this location. A surge of water nearly 30 feet high, and bristling with debris, roared downstream. When the flood crashed through the moraine, it dropped debris in the shape of a fan.

Unfortunately, even though there was adequate warning that the flood was raging down the valley, three campers at Aspenglen Campground were killed and $26 million damage was wrecked on downtown Estes Park.

Signs along the boardwalk expain the lives of beaver

~ 25 ~ Beaver Ponds Boardwalk

B eaver Ponds Boardwalk is a quarter-mile trail installed by the Park Service many years ago to allow visitors to experience a beaver-made habitat in a riparian ecosystem.

One of the things beavers do, sort of like humans, is move on. So whether they migrated upstream or down, the beavers who built here have migrated.

Much of the work they built remains. Notice the piles of branches laying in the water. These are small dams or remains of lodges. There are many sharp-pointed aspen stumps about, evidence of the beaver's hard work. They chew the trunk through, then disassemble the tree a piece at a time and take the wood where it's needed to keep damns and lodges intact.

The twists and turns of Hidden Valley Creek still fill with water. Though the dams do need some attention, they still hold enough runoff to fill many of the tiny lakes with water. Here you'll see a full bore riparian ecosystem. That is to say a wet, river valley teeming with birds, ducks, and hundreds of bug species, as well as all the water-loving plants that thrive here such as alder, birch, and willow.

A number of easy-to-read signs explain the goings-on of the beavers and all about the ecosystem. A word to the wise: apply a layer of mosquito repellent before venturing out of the car.

Right: Lake Haiyaha

Rocky is rife with wildlife and many of the species which the park supports may be seen on these hikes. Here is some information on the animals you are most likely to see in Rocky Mountain National Park.

Bighorn Sheep

These sturdy animals live among the rocks at many elevations in Rocky. They have true horns—which don't shed as an elk's antlers will. They have a gray to brown coat and tend to herd in loose groups. Sheep get to be about three feet tall and can tip the scales from 100 to 200 pounds. They eat a lot of different food types and like to eat in the morning and chew the cud from their many stomachs during the day. They have special hoofs which allow them to live among the rocks. The ones with the curlicue horns are males, female's horns are shorter and spikier.

Spot them at The Crater or among the rocks across the highway from Lake Irene.

Coyote

These solo mammals are found throughout the park. They hunt for small mammals and are easiest to find in grassy areas around sunrise and sunset. You often hear their howl if you are on a trail near sunset.

The Coyote Valley Trail and near the Moraine Park Museum are good spots for seeing these pretty animals.

Elk

These majestic creatures are common in Rocky Mountain National Park. These animals love to graze morning and evening and rest during the remainder of the day. A bull elk can weigh up to 1,000 pounds and have a set of antlers with a five-foot-wide spread. They drop the antlers every year and females never grow them. In the autumn the males "bugle" in a mating ritual which brings hundreds of visitors to the park to hear them.

Find them in autumn in Horseshoe Park and Moraine Park, and they love the golf course in Estes Park. In summer, look for them at higher elevations. Look for brown "lumps" as you walk Old Ute Trail or drive along Trail Ridge Road.

Mule Deer

These mammals can weigh in at 200 pounds. Their mule-like ears are a giveaway. The eat many grasses and undergrowth varieties.

Check out Cascade Falls, Ouzel Falls, Mill Creek Basin, Lulu City and East Inlet Meadows trails.

Black Bear

Truthfully, bear sightings are rare in Rocky though approximately 30–45 live in the park. They migrate from the low country to the higher and are most likely to be seen from afar.

They feed on nuts and berries mostly, though they eat meat opportunistically, reaching 200 to 600 pounds.

Abert's Squirrel

Keep an eye open for the tufted ears and brown coat of these active mammals. They stick to areas of ponderosa pine forest.

Look for these critters on the Moraine Park Nature Trail, right behind the museum, and along the first half-mile of Mill Creek Basin.

Beaver

Only humans affect their habitats as drastically as beavers. These busy bodies are in constant motion building and repairing their projects. They dam a stream then build a lodge in the middle of the lake created to protect themselves from their predators. The lodge is actually dry inside because its floor is higher than the water. Beavers mate for life, bearing young two or three at a time.

Look for them at East Inlet Meadows Trail, and Big Meadows.

Yellow-bellied marmots

Look for these whistling wonders wherever there is a pile of rocks, particularly above timberline. They hibernate for many months a year and consequently need a lot of food for their weight. You are quite likely to find them begging.

Scan for these at Rock Cut, Lulu City, and Old Ute Trail.

Golden-mantled ground squirrels

These are the chatteringly busy critters you'll find deep in the woods on all the forested trails of Rocky. Look for their distinctive stripes and golden color.

You might spot this species at Copeland Falls, East Portal/YMCA,, Lulu City, Coyote Valley.

As part of its ongoing educational programming, the rangers of Rocky Mountain National Park offer a number of guided hikes and walks. For up-to-the-minute information about days and time check at any ranger station or pick up a copy of *High Country Headlines*, the park's newspaper. Bring warm clothes, sturdy shoes, water and rain gear.

On the East Side of Rocky

Lily Lake Nature Walk
This stroll around Lily Lake explores the blend of natural and historical aspects of this pretty lake. The trail is entirely accessible with no elevation gain.

Park Ranger

Monday and Friday afternoons, Thursday mornings. Begins at the Lily Lake parking lot.

Moraine Park Nature Walk
Meet at the Moraine Park Museum for this half-mile, one-hour walk which explores the landscape and geology, flora and fauna, birds and bugs of Moraine Park. This walk goes every morning, Monday through Friday.

Tundra Nature Walk
Be sure to wiggle into some warm and wind-resistant clothes for this walk above timberline. Begins at Alpine Visitor Center several days per week. Explore the tiny plants, perhaps see elk, pica and yellow-bellied marmots.

Tyndall Gorge Walk
Explore Rocky's spectacular glacial landscape and lush alpine forest as nature prepares for winter. Meet at Bear Lake parking area for this one-and-a-half hour walk. It goes three days per week.

Western History Walk
On Saturdays and Sundays, rangers guide an easy, one-hour, two-part walk which explores the history of Moraine Park. Meets at the Moraine Park Museum.

Various Hikes
Each year the rangers select a unique lake or trail to take visitors to during regularly scheduled hikes. One year they chose The Lock, another Flattop Mountain. Check with any ranger or at any station about these ranger-led hikes.

On the West Side

Rocky Mountain Heritage Walk
Four afternoons per week rangers discuss the prehistory, Natives, miners and ranchers in the Rocky region. Explore the Old West at the historic Never Summer Ranch. One-mile and two-hours long, this walk starts at the Never Summer Ranch.

Alpine Experience
Meet at the flagpole of the Alpine Visitor Center to explore the Alpine tundra on this four-hour, four-mile walk. Dress warmly.

Colorado; Life along the River
Learn about the abundance of life thriving near the mighty Colorado. Meets at the Colorado River Trailhead; one-and-one-half miles; one-and-one-half hours.

Coyote Valley River Walk
This flat, one-hour walk explores the valley's ecology from the Coyoty Valley Trailhead.

Hells Hip Pocket
Climb to historic Grand Ditch on this strenuous, five-mile round-trip up into the Never Summer Mountains. Meets at Colorado River Trailhead.

Shipler Cabin Walk
Visit an early settlement in the Kawuneeche Valley. Learn about mining, trapping and early dude ranching. Five miles; four to five hours; moderate elevation gains.

Coyote Valley Night Walk
Meet at Coyote Valley trailhead for a night walk on this easy trail. Bring a flashlight.

Rock outcropping on Old Upper Ute Trail

~ 26 ~ Ute Trail

Fast Facts

Magnificent mountain vistas and tundra scenery

Length: 2.0 miles each way
Elevation Change: 150 feet
Map on Page: 50
Designation: Walk
Amenities: None
Trailhead: Parking pull off on the south side of Trail Ridge Road: Head up Trail Ridge Road. The pull-off is on the south side of Trail Ridge, 13 miles west of the Beaver Meadows entrance station. It is about 2 miles west of Rainbow Curve. If you reach Forest Canyon Overlook, you've gone too far. The trailhead is marked only by a small sign on the edge of a parallel parking area on the south side of Trail Ridge.

U tes and Arapahoe used the very trail you'll be walking to cross the Continental Divide.

Prepare for the elements of this easy but often cool and windy hike by dressing warmly in layers topped off with wind protection. The wind here is likely to be blowing the entire time you're walking. Some folks use ear plugs to quiet the noise, which helps to take the focus off any discomfort and puts it where it belongs, on the fantastic environment all around.

The trail begins at 11,440 feet above sea level; more than two miles. You are high above timberline as you head onto the clearly defined trail across a vast wildflower and rock strewn mountaintop. The trail sweeps across the breadth of tundra approaching Tombstone Ridge. The rocks there make interesting perches. Nearly 10 miles away rises Longs Peak. To the north unfurls the Mummy Range. One of the good things about this trail is that when you've had an eyeful of the eerie alpine beauty it offers, you simply turn around and head back to your car.

Look sharp for wildlife along this windblown trail. Yellow-bellied marmots and pica are as common as rocks, and ptarmigan are frequently spotted as well. Depending on the time of summer you visit and the local weather conditions the alpine tundra may be awash in wildflowers. The ground around you may be bursting with saxifrage, sedum and mountain dryad.

Left: Flattop Mountain

26
Ute Trail

27
Forest Canyon Overlook

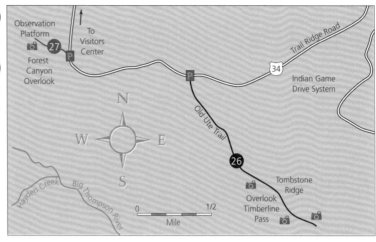

28
Rock Cut

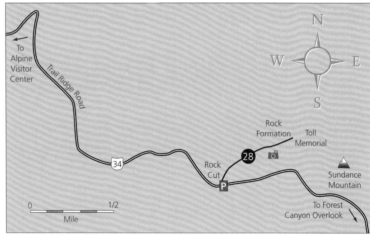

29
Fall River Pass

30
Alpine Ridge

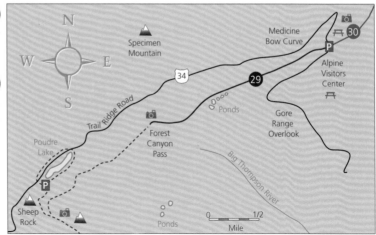

The overlook peers into Forest Canyon

~ 27 ~ Forest Canyon Overlook

It is common to see park visitors here dashing from their car to the overlook wearing only their T-shirts and shorts. Cold, they run to the overlook, take a quick peek and scurry back to their cars, unimpressed. But slip into something a bit warmer and turn the mad dash into a vista study for this is arguably the most scenic overlook in all of Rocky Mountain National Park.

The trail leaves the parking area and leads along a fence to the first overlook. Then it heads, dropping slightly to a second, even more dramatic, overlook.

Here you can see the heart of Rocky—Forest Canyon. The canyon had been carved into a "V"-shape by the Big Thompson River, which you see far below, then, thousands of years ago a glacier began to form upriver, to your right as you overlook the valley. It gained size and eventually filled the entire valley with flowing ice, carving the deep, "U"-shape you see today.

Beyond are a series of peaks. The seemingly nearest and most massive is Terra Tomah, with its vast, single, tundra slope. To the left is Stones Peak. The right is Mount Ida. The string of alpine lakes you see are called Gorge Lakes, for they set together in that gorge. This was solid rock at one time, carved out now by the shear force of moving ice. Far to the right you can make out the reddish hues of Specimen Mountain. And beyond, the Never Summer Mountains.

The Rock Cut Trail formations rise above Trail Ridge Road

~ 28 ~ Rock Cut Tundra Trail

Fast Facts

Fantastic rock formations and park-wide overviews

Length: 0.5 miles each way
Elevation Change: 250 feet
Map on Page: 50
Designation: Easy hike
Amenities: Restrooms
Trailhead: Rock Cut Trailhead Parking Lot: Take US 36 west out of Estes Park. Enter the park at Beaver Meadows entrance station and pass Deer Ridge Junction heading up Trail Ridge Road. The pull-off is on the east (right) side of Trail Ridge, approximatley 16 miles west of the Beaver Meadows entrance station.

There is a large parking lot here along with washroom facilities. As with all the tundra walks and easy hikes, the more you bundle up to stay warm, the more likely you are to enjoy the hike.

This trail gradually ascends to a bizarre, Stonehenge-like rock formation. It's hard to resist climbing them, but take care. Along the way a turn-off leads to other, weirder formations. These rocks are more than a billion years old. Probably the oldest rocks in the park they seem to have been part of the original Rocky Mountains, the ones which were formed and mostly eroded before the ones we see today were even born.

Hereabouts also notice the mountain peak finder which points out the names of the mountains you can see in every direction. The marker honors Roger Toll, who was the superintendent of Rocky throughout most of the 1920's. It was his idea to build Trail Ridge Road, connecting both sides of the park and offering some of the best sightseeing in the national park system.

You would have to go to northern Canada or Alaska to see as much tundra as you'll find in Rocky. Lots of flowers bloom along this trail: alpine avens, moss campion and tiny sunflower among hundreds of others.

The trail winds toward Fall River Pass

~ 29 ~ Fall River Pass

Fast Facts

Never Summer mountain views, tiny alpine tarns

Length: 2.0 miles each way
Elevation Change: -475 feet
Map on Page: 50
Designation: Walk
Amenities: Restrooms, restaurant, museum, gift shop
Trailhead: Alpine Visitor Center: From Estes Park take US Highway into the park and up Trail Ridge Road. The Alpine Visitor Center, one of the busiest spots in the park, is about 20 miles westerly from the Beaver Meadows entrance station. From Grand Lake take US Highway 34 into the park. The Alpine Visitor Center is about 21 miles from the Grand Lake entrance station.

The first two miles of this trail are the tundra portion of a longer trail which ends up going through some wonderful forest and past some interesting rock formations to finish at Poudre Lake. The first two miles are beautiful enough, though, to attract many walkers.

The trail begins directly across from the parking lot of the Alpine Visitor Center. Watch carefully for traffic, drivers tend to be watching the scenery, not the road.

No signage of any kind marks this trail, but once across the highway you can't miss it. You see it rolling toward a swell on the horizon. Above to your left you see Trail Ridge Road and on the right, too, you can see this superlative roadway snaking down.

Follow the trail as far as you like, enjoying the views of the Never Summer mountains and the spectacular red flanks of Specimen Mountain. As you walk along you may ask yourself, is there more? In fact, as the trail stretches out it seems to call to you to cross each successive hillock. If you continue, you will eventually reach a group of alpine lakes and a long, downstream view of Forest Canyon.

More!
The fact that this hike is downhill from the Alpine Visitor Center all the way to Poudre Lake makes it a natural for a shuttle hike; one group hikes while others shuttle the car to the pickup point at Poudre Lake.

Riparian Habitat

Situated along streams, rivers, lakes and ponds, riparian regions are lush areas which occur in both lower and higher elevations. Various shrubs—mountain and plane-leaf willow, river and dwarf birch and alder—thrive along well-watered shores. Beavers are the signature animal of these areas, althought other mammals such as muskrats, river otters, raccoons, shrews and voles also call it home. Wildflowers abound, including chiming bells, mountain woodlillies and °white bog orchids. Birds nest and hunt here: American snipers, sparrows, and ducks.

Montane Habitat

Occurring between 6,000 and 9,500 feet in elevation, montane forests are relatively open terrain. Ponderosa pine prefer the sunny, dry, south-facing slopes, whereas Douglas fir populate moister, north-facing flanks. Lodgepole pine and aspen grow throughout the environment, often indicating areas of disturbance such as fire or avalanche, since both are quick to pioneer newly exposed terrain.

While many types of plants and animals range across the Montane ecosystem, each tree type harbors communities which favor its company. Ponderosa parklands, for example, are the exclusive home of the Abert's squirrel, although mule deer, coyotes, striped skunks, elk and porcupine also frequent the territory. Douglas fir are often interspersed with lodgepole pine, creating dense woodlands with thin understory environments. Shade-tolerant shrubs and flowers—

Alpine Tundra

common juniper, mountain maple, smooth asters, fairy slippers, dwarf mistletoe—shelter pine martens and red squirrels. Aspen glens are, perfect for underbrush such as serviceberry, chokecherry and wild rose. Silvery lupines, yarrow and Colorado columbines dot the sunny areas where masked shrew hunt and birds such as Cordilleran flycatchers, violet-green swallows and woodpeckers dart from branch to branch.

Subalpine Forest

Engelmann spruce and subalpine fir form dense forests from 9,500 to 11,500 feet. In disturbed areas, stands of aspen and lodgepole pine are common and on exposed rocky ridges, limber pine thrive. In the upper reaches, stunted, malformed trees called krummholz (German for "crooked wood") display the effects of strong winds studded with ice crystals. Heavy accumulations of snow and slow

snowmelt keep the region moist. In the dark understory of the forest grow blueberries, huckleberries, and elderberries interspersed with Jacob's ladder, red columbine and heart-leaved arnica.

Least Chipmunks and long-tailed weasels favor this cool environment, alive with the rustles, chirps and warbles of blue grouse, mountain chickadees, dark-eyed juncos and ruby-crowned kinglets.

Elk and mule deer are common. Although this is their habitat, it is rare to come across black bears, lynx or wolverines.

Alpine Tundra

Above 13,500 feet trees disappear, giving way to an Arctic-like environment characterized by expanses of low-growing plants and fields of stone. This is the alpine tundra, where vegetation and animals must survive nearly 10 months of winter, often accompanied by hurricane-force winds. It is far from a barren land, however. The short summer bursts into life with tufts of marsh marigolds, alpine phlox and fairy primrose, accented by grasses and lichens. Butterflies, such as high mountain blues and Magdelena alpines seem too frail to occupy the windswept mountaintops, yet they thrive. Horned larks and white-tailed ptarmigans also do well, staying clear of the hooves of elk and bighorn sheep or the busy antics of pika and yellow-bellied marmots.

Vista of the park's north region from the end of the trail

~ 30 ~ Alpine Ridge

Fast Facts

360-degree views reaching as far as the Medicine Bow mountains of Wyoming

Length: 0.5 miles each way
Elevation Change: 150 feet
Map on Page: 50
Designation: Hike
Amenities: Restrooms, restaurant, museum, gift shop
Trailhead: Alpine Visitor Center: From Estes Park take US Highway into the park and up Trail Ridge Road. The Alpine Visitor Center, one of the busiest spots in the park, is about 20 miles westerly from the Beaver Meadows entrance station. From Grand Lake take US Highway 34 into the park. The Alpine Visitor Center is about 21 miles from the Grand Lake entrance station.

This trail has a number of names, "Stairway to Heaven," "Fall River Pass Tundra Trail" and "Huffers Hill" to list three, but by any name you can't help but find it. Park the car in the visitors center parking lot and there it is, a hundred or so steps calling out to be conquered.

The steps do seem steep. Take them slowly and stop several times for a breath of the fresh air and a long sip of water. From the rocks at the top of the stairway you can see more than 60 square miles of alpine tundra. A marker reminds you that you're higher than "famed" Mount Hood in Oregon. You are surrounded by true giants: the Mummy Range to your east, north lie Wyoming's Medicine Bows and to the west Colorado's Never Summer Range.

The trail takes a plunge north to a sign which overlooks the Cache la Poudre Valley, so named because French trappers left a cache of gunpowder near what became Ft. Collins, Colorado.

A museum has displays about the land above timberline—the alpine tundra—and several overlooks invite you to step up and admire the glacial bowl which the center overlooks. This is a cirque, gouged out by the beginnings of a glacier. Elk are frequently found among the bushes in the bottom of this bowl. Simply let your eyes adjust to the distance and search for brown lumps; elk tend to be laying down most of the day.

Overleaf: The Mummy Range from the alpine tundra of Ute Trail

Along the edge of The Crater

~ 31 ~ The Crater

Fast Facts

Hike to the edge of a glacial bowl with an opportunity to see bighorn sheep

Length: 1.0 miles each way
Elevation Change: 730 feet
Map on Page: 59
Designation: Hike
Amenities: None
Trailhead: The Crater Trailhead: The Crater trailhead is really a pullout with parking on the north side of Trail Ridge Road located approximately 4.0 miles west of the Alpine Visitor Center on Trail Ridge Road. It is 17 miles from the Grand Lake entrance station.

A few words about this hike. The Crater is one of the few remaining lambing areas for bighorn sheep left in Rocky Mountain National Park. Because these animals do their lambing in the spring months, this trail is closed from May 1 usually until the middle of July. If the trail is closed, please respect the park's decision and choose another hike.

The walk to The Crater is one of the most arduous described in this book because of its steepness over such a short distance. First the trail crosses a lush little meadow before heading into a sub-alpine forest for the next three-quarters-of-a-mile. Up and up it goes, switching back and forth. This trail can be hard work. Many folks sit for a rest along the trunks that have fallen by the side of trail.

Just when you don't think you can turn one more switchback you see light at the end of the forest. In this case that light is probably sunshine dancing across Specimen Mountain. The trail comes out of the woods into a wide-open area bounded by Specimen, the Crater's edge and the valley you've just climbed out of—the Cache la Poudre. Stop for a moment and turn around. Behind you, you can see Trail Ridge Road weaving up to the Alpine Visitor Center.

The path curls on up through the krummholz trees and into the tundra itself. Soon it crests a saddle and you see The Crater scooped out beneath you. Literally breath-

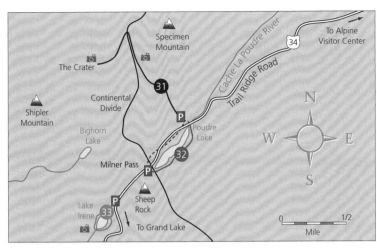

The Crater

32

Poudre Lake Walk

33

Lake Irene

taking, most folks stop and sit on a rock to admire the sculptural beauty of this bowl who's edge sweeps up to become a mountain. The mountain you see on the other side is Shipler Mountain. You are at 11,500 feet; Shipler's peak is 200 feet below you.

Chances are actually not that good of seeing a sheep here. The park wisely closes this trail when they are here. If you see the herd it is likely to be spread out among the rocks. Do not approach them. They need their space.

Carry Me: Essential items to pack on your hike

Whether you're headed for the quarter-mile, dead-level stroll around Sprague Lake or the seven-mile round trip to and from Lulu City being prepared is essential. Here is a list of items you'll find more than merely useful should trouble come your way.

- **Carry plenty of** water, more than you think you'll need. The air is dry in Rocky, and it's easy to get dehydrated. Take plenty of water and every time you think of taking a drink, take it. Take along some water treatment pellets as well in case you need to treat water from a stream or creek.
- **Carry food, too.** Walking burns calories, treat yourself to fresh fruit or trail mix. Not much in life beats stepping off the trail onto a rock with a view and noshing down a peanut butter and jelly sandwich.
- **Layers of clothing** are very important. Carry several layers which will enable you to warm up should cold weather pass over. And rain gear is absolutely necessary for those unexpected summer showers.
- **Sun screen protects** your skin from the harmful rays of the sun. Use it liberally. Lip balm is a good idea too. It prevents burned and dry, cracked lips.
- **Sun glasses prevent** your eyes from burning.
- **Insect repellent.** Rocky can be buggy.
- **Map or other** directions. Most of the trails in this book are on well-marked and well-maintained trails, but carrying a topographic map could be very helpful should you step off the trail for some reason and find yourself lost.
- **An all-purpose knife** with scissors and tweezers, and other attachments, can be very useful.
- **Matches, plenty of** them, in a waterproof carrying case.
- **A first aid kit**, either purchased or homemade, can help you out of a lot of jams.
- **A little toilet** paper will be a happily carried luxury should you find yourself in need. Bring along a plastic bag to carry the used tissue out.
- **A whistle and** a mirror may be helpful for signaling should you get lost.
- **Pack a flashlight**. And a couple extra batteries.

Poudre Lake atop the Continental Divide

~ 32 ~ Poudre Lake Walk

This is an easy stroll. First stop and have a look at the Continental Divide marker. As you face this, any rain falling to your right will end up in the Pacific Ocean via the Colorado River. And any rain falling to your left works its way into the Cache la Poudre River on to the mighty Mississippi and finally into the Gulf of Mexico. Needless to say, this is a very popular spot for photographing friends and family.

The trail itself is a paved walkway leading to the edge of the Poudre Lake. Walk down to the lake's edge and touch a hand in to see how cold the alpine waters really are. Avoid the temptation to drink the water, as pristine as it looks it may make you ill.

Follow the trail as far around the lake as you please. You take in pretty views of the lake settled into its mountainous bowl. You can make out several mountain ranges. As you walk along you begin to enter a subalpine forest ecosystem; tall trees, lots of moisture, and not much undergrowth. The trail eventually begins to climb toward Forest Canyon Pass.

Be on the lookout among the rocks for critters such as tiny pica and the ever-noisy yellow-bellied marmots. Birds include gray jays and ravens.

More!
Follow the trail into the trees on the far side of the lake. This uphill climb rewards with some fine vistas.

Lake Irene

~ 33 ~ Lake Irene

Fast Facts

A glacial lake offering an easy hike with many picnic opportunities

Length: 0.5 mile loop
Elevation Change: 60 feet
Map on Page: 59
Designation: Easy hike
Amenities: Restrooms
Trailhead: Lake Irene parking lot: The Lake Irene parking lot is located approximately 4.7 miles west of the Alpine Visitor Center on Trail Ridge Road. It is 16 miles from the Grand Lake entrance station. The parking lot is on the northwest side of the road, a right turn coming from Alpine Visitor Center; a left if coming from Grand Lake.

This is a quiet walk along a maintained gravel trail around a lovely lake high in the Rocky Mountains. Park in the lot and head for the downhill corner of the parking lot. A trail leads past some shady picnic benches. Follow this around a bend and you find yourself headed down a steep trail, very nearly a stairway. This is the steepest part of this hike.

Once you arrive at lake's shore stroll clockwise, gazing up to Shipler Mountain or down the Kawuneeche Valley. The walkway passes a marshy area and you cross Phantom Creek on a log bridge. The trail on the far side drifts through some trees and then runs very close to the lake itself. Closing the loop, the trail cuts uphill into trees and back to the parking lot past a cabin. An alternative spur near the parking lot leads deep into tall grass before crawling back up to that little cabin.

Lake Irene is often less crowded than more popular lakes in the park so it's a good place to plan a picnic.

As you leave the parking lot notice a tall, almost spire-like rock formation across the highway. This is a rare glacial feature called a *roches moutonnées*—a sheep rock. These rocks were too hard for the debris within a glacier to grind down. Often, though not here, they looked like the rounded backs of sheep. Ironically, the rock scree fields near this spire are a good place to look for Rocky Mountain bighorn sheep. This is a favorite summer hangout.

The mighty Colorado River is barely a stream near Lulu City

~ 34 ~ Lulu City

The trail begins up a small hill and heads north into the broad valley that holds the Colorado River. It actually does a lot of rolling along, gaining and losing much elevation as it snakes ever upstream. Unfortunately, the trail is rarely right along river's edge, it holds to the shoulder above the water. Through the occasional forest clearing you can see the Never Summer Mountains—and the trails ascending them—rising across the valley. For a long stretch you keep Shipler Mountain to your right. You can see Trail Ridge Road coursing into the distance and in another while you've passed into Shipler's shadow and realize you are deep in one of Rocky's wildest areas. The wide path, well maintained, passes through many miniature ecological zones:

One minute you're on a rock field, the next deep in a pine forest, suddenly you're in an aspen glen. As you pass rock fields on your right, stop to listen for the whistle-warnings of the yellow-bellied marmots. Pause to search them out as they poke their heads above the rocks.

The stream crosses a number of log bridges. After 2 miles spot Shipler cabin, or what's left of it. It's not much more than a pile of cut logs nowadays. But it's a great place for a rest and a bit of history exploring.

Eventually the trail turns east and climbs into a ravine. Then it rolls along until suddenly you emerge into an expansive wildflower-flecked

Along the trail to Lulu City

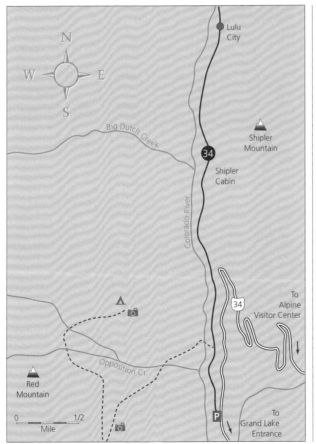

meadow. Don't miss the cabins of Lulu City just before the meadow, they show up on your right just after you ford across a sparkling little stream.

The meadow itself is one of the prettiest spots on the west side of Rocky Mountain National Park. It has terrific scenery of mountains all around and the waterway is as fresh and inviting as it must have been 120 years ago when people first came here.

As pretty as the valley is, and fresh as the water is, it's hard not to strip off your boots and socks to splash around in the water. Several footpaths lead to small gravel beaches at water's edge. The water is shockingly cold, even late in the summer, but decidedly refreshing.

Lulu City

Rangers conduct regular tours of the ranch

~ 35 ~ Never Summer Ranch

A wide, gravel road leads through gates and across the Colorado River. The bridge is a particularly good spot for a photograph with the river and the mountains in the background. After crossing the bridge the road curves and leads up to the Never Summer Ranch itself.

This rugged, old-style dude ranch sets in a clump of trees. Many of the log buildings are open to the public. The house itself has tiny rooms, you feel like a giant as you walk through. But it's interesting to see how folks lived day-to-day back at the turn of the last century. There is a taxidermy area and an ice storage room—sort of a walk in refrigerator. Usually, one or more of the cabins where the hired hands stayed are open as well. It's easy to see that life wasn't very glamorous for the people who occupied these mountain homes.

The Never Summer was actually an early dude ranch. A fellow named Johnny Holzwarth kept it going from the 1920s to the 1970s. The accommodations seem crude by today's standards, but guests in those days came expressly to experience that ruggedness. Mr. Holzwarth actually dedicated this land for preservation rather than accept hefty sale offers.

The trail heads into deep forest

~ 36 ~ Bowen/Baker Trail

Put this in the stroll category. You park your car in the lot and walk around the gate to follow the road into the wide-open spaces of the Kawuneeche Valley. After about a quarter-mile the road splits. Bear to the right circling around a lodgepole pine forest and passing a house. Eventually the road works its way back around the trees and you find yourself in a forest clearing used as a parking lot during hunting season.

Now we begin the most enjoyable part of this hike. The trail leads out of Rocky Mountain National Park into the Routt National Forest. And it sticks like glue to a bouncing, gurgling, happily rolling little stream. Follow this as long as you please, it starts its steep climb up Baker Gulch in about a quarter-of-a-mile.

This little hike has a lot of advantages. First, it is not well known and consequently likely to be deserted, even on holiday weekends. Second, while the views as you cross the valley aren't exceptional, the creek you follow at the end is as merry a little waterway as you'll find. There are many spots to stop and dip your feet in or sit on a log to contemplate the meaning of life or read a book while the kids play in the water. This is an excellent hike to do a bit of story-telling about the magical forest.

More!

Follow the trail as far up into the mountains as you please.

The Kawuneeche Valley from the Coyote Valley Trail

~ 37 ~ Coyote Valley Trail

Fast Facts

Incredible mountain vistas accompany a walk along the Colorado River. Explanatory markers explain the locale.

Length: 1.0 mile loop
Elevation Change: 0.0 feet
Map on Page: 70
Designation: Walk
Amenities: Restrooms, wheelchair accessible
Trailhead: Coyote Valley Trailhead: The Coyote Valley Trailhead parking lot is 5.9 miles north on US Highway 34 (Trail Ridge Road) from the Grand Lake entrance station. There is a small parking lot with restrooms.

This is one of the newest trails in the park. Its wide gravel design was laid out with ease of walking in mind along with some fantastic views and a touch of education thrown in. The trail leads out of the parking lot and immediately crosses the mighty Colorado—which makes some pretty turns here. After you cross the river you can bear left to some picnic tables or bear right to follow the path. Follow the path and you make a bee-line into the wide open riparian habitat of the Kawuneeche Valley. A spur leads down to the river itself, well worth exploring, and the main trail leads into a clump of trees half-a-mile away.

Here and there along this very pleasant walk benches are placed so you can have a rest and a drink of water.

Signage has been designed and installed to give you all the facts about the habitat, the geology, and the history of the area.

The Park Service must think they are having a little joke by calling this the Coyote Valley Trail. The valley we are in here is called the Kawuneeche Valley. This is an Indian word meaning coyote. So we are walking the coyote trail in the coyote valley.

Take this walk at dawn or dusk and you might see a coyote. You're quite likely to see deer and elk at those times of day. They love the grass that drapes the fields here. A pair of bald eagles has been sighted nearby. Look for them perching high in naked pine trees.

Right: Baker Mountain

Coyotes are common in Rocky

35
**Never Sum-
mer Ranch**

36
**Bowen/
Baker**

37
**Coyote
Valley**

38
**Big
Meadows**

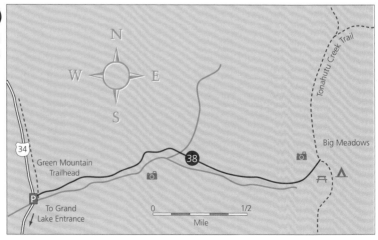

Tonahutu Creek in grassy Big Meadows

~ 38 ~ Big Meadows

Fast Facts

*A shaded forest trek rewards
with grass-filled,
high alpine meadows*

Length: 1.8 miles each way
Elevation Change: 600 feet
Map on Page: 70
Designation: Hike
Amenities: Restrooms
Trailhead: Green Mountain
Trailhead: The trailhead parking
lot is 2.8 miles north on US
Highway 34 (Trail Ridge Road)
from the Grand Lake entrance
station. There is a large parking
lot with restrooms.

You are actually taking the Green Mountain Trail as far as Big Meadows in this hike. The first half-mile is an uphill slog through pine forest. As interesting as the forest and groundcover are, the relentless uphill work does get tiresome, particularly along the many spots where horses have left souvenirs.

The trail levels off at a set of beaver ponds to the right and the same forest somehow becomes less monotonous.

This uphill work finally rewards with a long level trail leading east, deep into the park. After another half-mile the trail reaches a sharp turn and a horse hitch, you've reached the meadows. The actual trail bears right, but head out on the spur trail which leads straight ahead and downhill a bit and out into Big Meadow.

Here the forest opens up and you are in a vast, glacial valley swaying with grass. This valley was carved by ice thousands of years ago. Hop onto the rocks to raise your perspective so you can take it all in. As you come off the trail you are looking due east at Mount Patterson (11,424 feet). To your left, the meadow leads north, deep into Rocky's wilderness, to the right it runs southerly, heading directly for Grand Lake.

There are excellent picnic spots everywhere you look. Most overlook water features, too—eddies and pools of Tonahuto Creek. Ducks are common.

Go back to the trail and

Golden Banner

follow it as far as you like as it skirts the meadows in the trees. Another spur trail leads across the meadow to the Big Meadows Campground. A little exploring rewards with a lot of bird and bug sightings.

More!

After this trail reaches Big Meadows you can follow the trail downstream and right along the creek. Arrange with friends or family for a pick up at the Kawuneeche Visitor

Center. This will add almost 4 miles, most of it down hill, some of it very scenic and some of it through dense, featureless forest.

Trees

Aspen

Also called quaking aspen because the leaves are so light they rotate in any little puff of mountain air, these common trees grow in clumps in montane ecosystems throughout the west. They have whitish bark—often marred with human initials—and their leaves turn spectacular colors come autumn.

Ponderosa pine

These irregularly shaped trees have a gnarled, red bark and do not have a pointed or conical top. They prefer south-facing grassy areas in the Montane zone.

Douglas fir

Where you see Ponderosa pine, look across the valley and you'll likely find these straight trunks. They prefer the moister, cooler

Aspen in autumn

north facing side of the same valley as the Ponderosa.

Lodgepole pine

These grow at slightly higher elevations and often without much undergrowth. The trunks are as straight as lodge poles, and they grow to 90 or more feet.

Subalpine fir

These are so common in the subalpine ecosystem as to share the name. They love the moisture provided by deep snow so prefer higher elevations. Silvery bark wraps a large-diameter trunk growing to up to 80 feet tall.

Engelmann spruce

These love the elevations from about 9,500 to treeline. In fact, most of the "banner" trees you see are windblown Engelmann spruce.

Mule deer along the trail

Blue Grouse

~ 39 ~ Summerland Park

The Summerland Park trail is really the gravel road which leads out of the parking lot through a gate. It drops about 50 feet right away, thus accomplishing all the elevation loss and gain for this hike in its first few yards.

This country gravel road heads straight along between a tree-covered ridge and a series of fields. Watch your step, there are potholes and horse droppings aplenty on this well-used road. A split log fence separates you from the grassy meadows. You are right on one of Rocky's southern borders and the land beyond the fence is private. The horses which are often there compose a classic picture with Mount Enentah in the background.

Gradually the road begins to curve and weave a little and you find yourself among trees passing a house. Head on and in a few steps you are in Summerland Park. You know you're there when you see North Inlet bending right up to the road beneath your feet.

To your left stretches out Summerland Park itself, a wide open meadow filled with possibilities for in-the-wild entertainment. There are trees to climb, a stream to play in, and picnic tables.

More!

Follow the trail another 2.3 miles (and 250 feet of elevation) through some very fine aspen and pine forest to Cascade Falls (Hike 40).

Water Lilies

39
Summerland Park

40
Cascade Falls

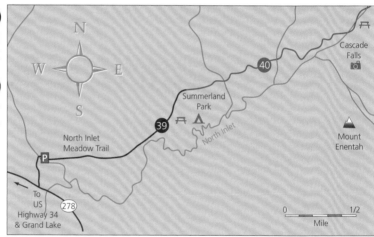

Cascade Falls

40

Summerland Park

39

North Inlet Meadow Trail

North Inlet

Mount Enentah

P

To US Highway 34 & Grand Lake

278

0   1/2
Mile

41
Adams Falls

42
East Inlet Meadows

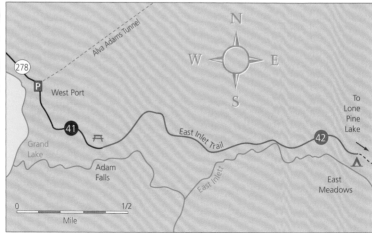

Alva Adams Tunnel

278

P   West Port

41

East Inlet Trail

42

To Lone Pine Lake

Grand Lake

Adam Falls

East Inlet

East Meadows

0   1/2
Mile

One of the many cascades

Gray Jay

~ 40 ~ Cascade Falls

Walk the road for 1.2 miles to Summerland Park. Stay on the trail which bears up to the left and into the trees. The way to Cascade falls is through aspen glen and lodgepole pine forest. The forest is dappled with thick undergrowth and the trail takes many turns out into the valley of the creek (the North Inlet) which offer fine vistas of the surrounding ridges and valleys.

Wildlife is thick. Once past Summerland Park the trail is very quiet. You are likely to see deer and a binocular study of the meadows along the creek may reveal moose. Re-introduced several years ago, they are thriving hereabouts now.

Gradually the trail begins to climb as it curls around Nisa and Patterson Mountains. You hear the falls before you reach them. The lookout from the trail gives barely a glimpse. To experience them you must carefully head off trail, scrambling down piles of rocks until you see them. Be very cautious should you choose to do this. Be very careful not to twist an ankle or put out a knee. The rocks can be slippery.

Cascade Falls is a rush of water dropping about 100 feet, but not in a single drop, it cascades down piles and piles of rocks.

More!

Follow the trail along as far as you like. Eventually it becomes a strenuous hike for miles and miles around many mountains back to Grand Lake. This is one for expert hikers.

Adam's Falls

A misty morning

~ 41 ~ Adam's Falls

Fast Facts

A short hike in alpine forest to a waterfall

Length: 0.3 miles each way
Elevation Change: 79 feet
Map on Page: 74
Designation: Easy hike
Amenities: Restrooms
Trailhead: East Inlet Trailhead: The trailhead is located near the West Portal of the Alva Adams Tunnel. Take any cross street from Lake Avenue (the main street) in Grand Lake away from the lake to West Portal Road. Turn right (east) until you reach the well-signed turnoff. This is a left turn into a parking lot.

The trail heads out of the parking lot along a log fence and quickly reaches the forest. Walk along, climbing a bit, descending a bit, until you reach the sign, which guides you to take a right turn to Adams Falls. Follow the trail through mixed aspen and pine forest until you scramble across house-size boulders for a look at these water wonders.

The water here doesn't drop far, perhaps 50 feet, but the hardness of the rock has forced the water into a narrow wedge which makes it particularly pretty.

The park recently installed a sort of viewing platform because people kept crawling onto the rocks and falling into the creek—quite a drop. For maximum safety stay on the trail at all times.

More!
Continue on for Hike Forty Two, East Inlet Meadow Trail

Muledeer

East Inlet Creek

~ 42 ~ East Inlet Meadow Trail

Fast Facts

Adam's Falls, broad meadows ringed with mountains, waterfalls and possibly moose

Length: 1.7 miles each way
Elevation Change: 160 feet
Map on Page: 74
Designation: Hike
Amenities: Restrooms
Trailhead: East Inlet Trailhead: The trailhead is located near the West Portal of the Alva Adams tunnel. Take any cross street from Lake Avenue (the main street) in Grand Lake away from the lake to West Portal Road. Turn right (east) until you reach the well signed turnoff. This is a left turn into a parking lot.

The first third mile of this trail coincides with the Adam's Falls trail. Be sure to head up to those falls before you walk up into the meadow.

The trail climbs into mixed forest of aspen, Douglas fir, lodgepole pine and Engelmann spruce. In spots the trail is fairly rocky. This trail comes out of the forest frequently to overlook the entire valley. As you step out of the trees onto one of these intimate overlooks the East Meadow, a glacially carved "park." East Inlet Creek loops and winds past. The mountain you see is named Mount Craig, but you instantly understand why locals call it Mount Baldy.

This hike is high on list of places you are most likely to see moose in Rocky. Hike early in the morning for the best opportunities. They are likely to be among the acres of willow bush which crowd the creek. Take binoculars and scan for them from the trail's many overlooks. You're likely to come up with beaver and muskrat sightings as well.

East Inlet Meadows Trail winds its way up and down the shoulders of Mount Enentah and Mount Cairns, rising 30 feet, dropping 30, twisting mountainward, torquing meadow-ward until it reaches the east end of this 2-mile-long meadow.

More!
Head up the steep switchbacks past the falls toward Lake Verna. This adds five miles and over 1,700 feet of gain.

Wildflower

Alpine wildflowers

Colorado clouds

Cowpokes and customers near Sprague Lake

Family at play on the Colorado River

Bird

Douglas fir tree

Ranger-guided bug hunt in the Big Thompson River

Right: Elk graze in the Kawuneeche Valley

Patrick Soran

Writer, photographer, architect Patrick Soran, a native Coloradan, first went to Rocky Mountain National Park with his parents when he was five years old. He has a clear memory of playing in the Colorado River in his underwear, but he wants you to know that he didn't do anything in there that any five year old wouldn't have.

For several years Patrick studied design, receiving a Master of Architecture from the University of Colorado in 1982 and his license to practice in Colorado in 1984. For ten years he designed luxury homes and hotel and restaurant interiors around the United States.

In the early 1990's he took a weekend travel writing class on a lark but within a week he had purchased a computer and camera to pursue what quickly became his dream job—traveling to exotic destinations and writing about the people and adventures he discovered there for newspapers and magazines.

Over the years, Patrick has written hundreds of articles about travel, design and architecture.

This is Patrick's fourth title for Altitude Publishing. He is also the co-author of the Colorado SuperGuide (third printing), the Rocky Mountain National Park SuperGuide and Colorado—A History in Photographs (second printing).

Patrick lives in Denver, Colorado where he enjoys running, hiking, getting out on his bicylce now and then and drinking coffee with friends.

Dedication

For Dan forever. And Stephen. And Jim and Jim and James and Jimmy and Kuma. And Terry. And Don. And lately, and fondly, Tomas.

Reference

ROCKY MOUNTAIN NATIONAL PARK

Rocky Mountain National Park, Estes Park, CO 80517; call 970/ 586-1206

EMERGENCIES

Dial 911 to reach local emergency services. The Estes Park Medical Center is a fully-staffed hospital with 24-hour emergency service; call 970/ 586-2317. The Grand Lake Medical can be reached at 970/ 627-8477.

FEDERAL AGENCIES

Bureau of Land Management, Colorado State Office, 2850 Youngfield St., Lakewood, CO 80215; call 303/ 239-3600.

U.S. Fish & Wildlife Service, P.O. Box 25486, DFC, Denver, CO 80225; call 303/ 236-7904.

U.S. Forest Service, P.O. Box 25127. Lakewood, CO 80225; call 303/ 275-5350.

U.S. Geological Survey, Box 25046 Federal Center, Mail Stop 504, Denver, CO 80225-0046; call 303/ 202-4200.

COLORADO INFORMATION

Colorado Travel & Tourism Authority, P.O. Box 22005, Denver, CO 80222; call 800/ COLORADO; internet http://www.colorado.com.